Rethinking the Western Tradition

*The volumes in this series
seek to address the present debate
over the Western tradition
by reprinting key works of
that tradition along with essays
that evaluate each text from
different perspectives.*

The Prince

NICCOLÒ MACHIAVELLI

Translated and edited

by

Angelo M. Codevilla

Commentary by

William B. Allen

Hadley Arkes

Carnes Lord

Yale University Press

New Haven & London

Published with assistance from the foundation
established in memory of Philip Hamilton McMillan
of the Class of 1894, Yale College.

Set in Times Roman type by
Keystone Typesetting, Inc.,
Orwigsburg, Pennsylvania.
Printed in the United States of America by Vail-Ballou Press,
Binghamton, New York.

Library of Congress Cataloging-in-Publication Data
Machiavelli, Niccolò, 1469–1527.
[Principe, English]
The prince / Niccolò Machiavelli ; translated and edited by Angelo M.
Codevilla ; commentary by William B. Allen, Hadley Arkes, Carnes Lord.
p. cm. — (Rethinking the Western tradition)
Translated from the Italian.
Includes bibliographical references and index.
ISBN 0-300-06402-0 (alk. paper). —
ISBN 0-300-06403-9 (paper : alk. paper)
1. Political science — Early works to 1800.   2. Political ethics.
I. Codevilla, Angelo, 1943-   .   II. Allen, William B.   III. Arkes,
Hadley.   IV. Lord, Carnes.   V. Title.   VI. Series.
JC143.M3813   1997
320.1 — dc21   9650047
                                              CIP

A catalogue record for this book is available from the
British Library.

The paper in this book meets the guidelines for
permanence and durability of the Committee on
Production Guidelines for Book Longevity of the
Council on Library Resources.

10 9 8 7 6 5 4 3 2 1

Contents

Editor's Introduction

Why did *The Prince* become the fountainhead of modern political thought? Why have so many people cursed it, praised it, argued about it for half a millennium? By the time it was printed, in 1532, almost twenty years after it was written, the controversies that had most stirred the author and were the book's liveliest examples had become yesterday's news to Italians. For readers ever since, the quarrels of Florence circa 1500 have been less interesting than those of ancient Greece or Rome. But perceptive readers have always known that this little book is about much more than the events it describes.

Like all great books, *The Prince* is written on several levels. On the most obvious level, it talks about various ways of organizing government, explains that Italian rulers do not know well enough how to organize armed support, gives some practical hints about how to do that, and tells the prince that the sooner he follows the advice the better off Italy will be.

On a deeper level, *The Prince* aims to teach the art of government to people regardless of where or when they live. Machiavelli gives lots of illustrated teachings about the instrumental role of religion in politics, about the need to get along with enemies or put them out of action, about the superior trustworthiness of weak allies. Together, these maxims add up to what came to be known (much later) as realpolitik. Although some decried the harshness and amorality of the book and most sought practical advice from it, still others thought that Machiavelli's practical maxims freed us all from the myth that government is about the pursuit of goodness. Armed with the knowledge that princes are irreducibly selfish, ordinary people could protect their own interests by limiting the power of government. Thus Jean-Jacques Rousseau wrote that *The Prince* is really the handbook of antimonarchists. And, in fact, much of the Western constitutional tradition consists of attempts to safeguard the good of individuals by counterposing society's various selfish tendencies.

On the deepest level of all, *The Prince* began the most recent and most revolutionary chapter of the central controversy of our civilization, namely, are our concepts of right and wrong merely reflections of our interests and power or do they reflect, however hazily, the objective order of things, whether natural or divine? Machiavelli took the side of those ancients who had argued, along with Plato's Thrasymachus, that "justice is the interest of the stronger." More significantly, he did so by foreclosing the very consideration that anything might be more important than triumph in struggles for power. By images rather than argument, he showed the absolute primacy of self-interest and dictated that people establish values to help them win. All modern political thought flows from this insight, articulated most clearly in Chapter XV of *The Prince*. This insight — usefulness is the only objective reality, the interests of human beings are inherently incompatible, the nonexistence of God means that earthly power is absolute — is the reason why Christians have stigmatized Machiavelli as a teacher of evil. It is why Thomas Hobbes, G. W. F. Hegel, Auguste Comte, and countless lesser lights have used Machiavelli as their compass.

In sum, modern government — its sovereign amorality, its huge size, the interest-group politics within it — can be explained only in terms of Machiavelli's ideas.

Thus *The Prince* is not a handbook for wielding power in a bygone time. It is a key part of our civilization's debate about how human beings get along with one another. Its teachings — from the obviously true about the relationship of military organization to political power, to the sometimes true–sometimes ruinous political advice, to the philosophical "new modes and orders" — are essential to understanding Machiavelli's time, our own, and all others as well.

In 1494, when Niccolò Machiavelli was twenty-five years old, King Charles VIII of France invaded Italy. This ended some seven hundred years of relative peace and independence. Foreign rule would last for the next four hundred years, and Italy would not again know a half-century of peace until our own time. What happened? During the Middle Ages, Italian cities had enjoyed much independence from the Holy Roman Emperor, from the pope, and from one another. Italian canon lawyers were prominent throughout Christendom, and Italian traders reached the far corners of the known world. Then the Turks advanced in the Balkans, shut down the old Western terminals of the Silk Road from China, and took Constantinople. Meanwhile, French and Spanish kings subdued their vassals, built big standing armies, and paid much less attention to Italian lawyers. The major Italian cities, Venice, Milan, and Florence, tried to make up for lost influence abroad by pulling their smaller neighbors into their little empires. Venice needed land to cultivate the mulberry trees to feed the silkworms to make the silk it could no longer get cheaply from China. Milan's Visconti family and Florence's Medicis were after more pomp and power. The Pope's Rome, too, carved out its little empire in central Italy. As wars between Venice, Milan, Florence, and Rome raged, it was inevitable that one side would call for help from abroad. Venice did it first, then everyone else did as well. When the foreign troops came, they outclassed the mercenaries on whom the Italian cities relied. Florence was one of the losers in 1494, and its ruling Medici family was overthrown. A republic was established, run until 1498 by Girolamo Savonarola, a friar who pushed repentance and ended by being burned at the stake, and between 1502 and 1512, by Pietro Soderini, a rich man who was not terribly bright or energetic.

In 1498, the young Machiavelli began a fourteen-year career of service to the republic. As a diplomat, Machiavelli observed how France had become such a military power, namely, by replacing medieval levies with the long-term professional *compagnies d'ordonnance* — the core of what became the French army. He was also struck by Cesare Borgia's conquest of the Romagna region, east of Florence, by ruthless management of alliances. Machiavelli's dispatches urge imitating both France and Borgia. The biggest practical undertaking of Machiavelli's career, from 1504 to 1512, was precisely to promote, to organize, and to recruit the Florentine version of the French army, which he called *Ordinanza*. Years later, his ribald comedy *La mandragola* (1520) was an allegory on the campaign to get the city to adopt his scheme. Adopt it Florence did. But when the battle of Prato (1512) put the little army to the test, it broke and ran. The Florentine Republic was defeated, the Medicis resumed power, and Machiavelli, among others, was out of a job and in jail.

When he got out, it took him less than six months to write *The Prince*. Any policy analyst reading it would note its policy prescriptions. Above all, any prince or republic that wants to prevail must have armed forces that are its own in every possible way. Soldiers and citizens must be one and the same. The prince, or the republic's leading men, must command the troops personally and must do whatever it takes to keep the troops happy and devoted. The foundation of political power is the willingness of an army to fight and win. Nothing substitutes for that. Technical devices such as fortresses may be useful or not, depending on circumstances. Religion can help, if it reinforces the will to fight. Laws and constitutions too are of secondary importance, because "where there are good arms there must be good laws." As for allies, their availability is inversely proportional to the need for them: "Whoever has good arms will always have good friends."

So, like the king of France and lots of other winners, make the army your own, make it good, and never stop thinking about how to use it. Second, always remember that power is not the main thing, it is the only thing. If you do that, you will be able to take advantage of whatever breaks you get, like Cesare Borgia, Hannibal, Agathocles, and other winners. That means getting competitors off their guard and then defeating them utterly. By helping the weak against the strong, you diminish the number of competitors you need fear. Whatever you do, do not bring someone more powerful than yourself into your quarrel, lest you lose your independence.

These prescriptions are sound, but hardly original. Others had noted the importance of armies and of the singleminded pursuit of power. Some, such as Francesco Guicciardini, had done so in writing just as well as Machiavelli, and practiced their prescriptions better. Whereas Guicciardini successfully ran Romagna for Pope Julius II, Machiavelli's new model army flunked the decisive test of battle against Spanish troops. Machiavelli was also a failure at keeping his eye on the ball. In 1520, after having begged the Medici family for seven years, he got a job so minor that he felt humiliated. Yet the job marked him as a traitor to the Republican cause. When the Medicis were thrown out again in 1526, the new republic did not deem Machiavelli important enough to punish. Had *The Prince* been primarily about Florentine policy, the world would have forgotten it more quickly than it did the works of Guicciardini.

The Prince, however, is full of pithy maxims about how anybody anywhere can succeed. Guidebooks to success have always been popular. Attentive readers discovered that Machiavelli's maxims together teach a certain style of government. Like any popular how-to book, *The Prince* has something for everyone. Those who want to defend against conspiracies get obviously good advice — never leave anyone in a position to hurt you who may have any reason to hurt you. They also get advice that is probably sound — make sure that those who rule others on your behalf will be strangers to the people they rule. But the book also gives plenty of good advice to conspirators — tell no one of your plans unless and until the other person has no choice but to join you or die. Like all how-to books, however, *The Prince* offers advice that is common sense and easier given than put into practice. Indeed, the advice often seems contradictory. For every example of efficacious cruelty (the Roman emperor Severus), there is one of cruelty that brings contempt and ruin (the emperor Commodius). For every example of a successful betrayer (Cesare Borgia), there is a traitor who comes to ruin

(Oliverotto da Fermo). So, on this level the standard charge that Machiavelli teaches people to do evil is only half true.

Sixteenth-century France attributed the cruelties and broken promises of King Henry IV to the alleged presence of a copy of *The Prince* by the bedside of his wife, Catherine de' Medici. There are rumors that Stalin himself read the book nightly. But surely neither Stalin nor Henry IV did their bloody deeds by following recipes. Nonetheless, both fit into Machiavelli's category of willful men who founded or refounded regimes. The whole practical point of *The Prince* is to persuade readers to imitate the likes of Stalin or Henry IV.

Why such emphasis on the founders of regimes? By asking this we begin to grasp why Machiavelli changed our civilization. For almost two thousand years before Machiavelli, our civilization's dominant thinkers — Plato, Aristotle, Cicero, Augustine, Aquinas — had judged political arrangements by the kind of human behavior they would produce. The point was to bring out the better side of humanity as much as circumstance would allow. Machiavelli's *Prince* is also full of maxims about human character, but they do not point the reader toward the improvement of character. All of us, princes and people, says Machiavelli, are alike in what matters most. We passionately love our lives and comforts. We will do anything, betray anyone, to escape death and poverty. We pledge our allegiance easily, but when redeeming our pledges becomes dangerous, we can't remember why we ever made them. We are likelier to forget the murder of our parents than an injury to our pocketbook. Anyone who forgets that men are this way will suffer. And if he then appeals to God, it will do him no good on earth. By painting this picture of "what men do," together with lively images of men who founded or refounded regimes by doing "what men do" better than just about everybody else, *The Prince* pointed readers toward a new kind of government.

That kind of government had already begun to take shape under Ferdinand and Isabella of Spain as well as under the French kings. But even in these countries, never mind in Italy, England, or Germany, legal-constitutional thought was still medieval. At least in theory, the primary political unit was still Christendom. Within it, every city, every guild, every king, duke, and the emperor and Church itself, had a place defined by law and custom. The place of each was disputable, but the notion that any member of the community might claim the right to do whatever he wished on a piece of territory — regulating economic life and religion, and even deciding what powers, if any, guilds and nobles might have — would have been considered megalomaniacal blasphemy. Only God was sovereign. And yet if Machiavelli's picture of "what men do" was accurate, the Spanish and French kings had not yet gone far enough in subduing the Church, in putting all administrative power into the hands of bureaucrats, in making military forces into their personal servants, and in reducing the nobles to idle rich.

Machiavelli's *Prince* was hardly the only influence in the rise of the modern state. Bloody struggles between Protestants and Catholics, superimposed on struggles for local autonomy and personal ambition, wracked Europe between the mid-sixteenth century and the mid-seventeenth century. The intellectual influence of *The Prince* on Western legal-constitutional thought during this period and for some time thereafter, however, is unmistakable. In 1576, in Paris, Jean Bodin published *The Six Books of the Republic*, in which he enunciated the concept of sovereignty. The king must be sovereign, even if he is not good, because other men are not good either. Constant struggle is intolerable internally and invites foreign rule. The king's power to rearrange and rule his realm could be limited by nothing on earth. Bodin built a constitutional structure fit for Machiavelli's prince. Thomas Hobbes's *Leviathan* (1651) used Machiavelli's premises about "what men do" to describe the reasons why non-princes would want to live as subjects of the modern sovereign state — because they would suffer less. Hugo Grotius's *On the Law of War and Peace* (1625) set forth the modern theory of relations between sovereign regimes that may destroy one another in war but may not otherwise challenge one another's supreme right to do whatever they want within their borders, because none is objectively better than any other, and none can be expected to recognize any authority higher than itself.

By the turn of the eighteenth century, Europe's primary practical problem had become to mitigate the power of absolute rulers. But although few constitutional thinkers at the time cited Machiavelli, most who worked on the problem did so from Machiavelli's premise about "what men do." John Locke's *Second Treatise* (1690) and Montesquieu's *Spirit of the Laws* (1714) were primary examples of what the authors of the United States Constitution called "the new political science," whose objective was to arrange social and governmental institutions to juxtapose human interests and passions. The artfully arranged clash of interests, making up for the defect of better motives, might yield pleasant living.

Clearly, mere pleasant living was not the objective of Machiavelli's *Prince*. Machiavelli wanted glory and empire. Nor did Machiavelli think that *real* rulers could be restrained by anything. The prospect of pleasant living may restrain some men, but nothing can restrain those who in Abraham Lincoln's words belong to "the family of the lion or the tribe of the eagle." Nor, within the bounds of Machiavelli's examples, can anything restrain corrupt or vicious men.

Of course, "what men do" at any given time depends on what habits they have acquired. In his famous debates with Lincoln, Stephen Douglas argued that he did not care whether the American people voted to allow slavery or to ban it. The essence of good government, said Douglas, is "popular sovereignty" — the majority's unfettered right to choose. Lincoln, however, said that if the people give in to the original sin of politics, that is, "you work, I'll eat," they will get into the habit of quarreling over who shall live off whom. The habit of disposing of innocent human lives for convenience's sake, said Lincoln, makes men unfit to govern themselves.

Hence, the problem of political life based on "what [Machiavellian] men do" is not easily dealt with. As we shall see, it is very much alive in our own time.

Machiavelli's *Prince* has had its most revolutionary influence on the most fundamental level of social thought. Those who have cursed *The Prince* most, and those who have praised it most, agree that the heart of the matter is Chapter XV. Here Machiavelli does something no one else had ever done: he creates his own set of values.

Since the fifth century B.C. a great dispute has been at the very center of our civilization. Socrates argued that right and wrong, better and worse, exist regardless of what anyone may think and that the presence of diverse opinions means they cannot all be correct. No amount of power or prominence can falsify something that is true, or make true something that is not. At his trial, Socrates acknowledged the Athenian people's lawful authority over his life but told them that they were wrong and that he would follow "the god," the truth, rather than them. By the same token, Jesus exhorted his followers: "Ye shall know the truth, and the truth shall make you free." On the other side of the controversy, Pontius Pilate asked Jesus rhetorically: "What is truth?" Similarly, Socrates' great antagonist in Plato's *Republic*, Thrasymachus, argued that right is the interest of the stronger — that the power of whoever gets to make the rules is the deepest truth and the only source of right.

The idea that something can be true and right even when it contradicts a nation's laws and mocks its customs and rulers, even when it jeopardizes a nation's safety is, was, and always will be inherently subversive. Athens put Socrates to death, and Rome resisted both Socratic philosophy and

Christianity because their affirmation of truths that transcend power challenged their authority. But when Rome decayed, Christianity and Socratic philosophy became the dominant intellectual forces in the West. For a thousand years after St. Augustine, only the nominalist movement challenged the notion that right and power are unrelated.

Machiavelli's intellectual rebellion was, above all, against what he called the "present religion." By this he meant that there had been religions before Christianity, there would be religions after it, and that he adhered to none. The Christian church claims to be the visible representative of the man who said, "I am the way, the truth, and the life." Socratic philosophy claims that the human mind can grasp the most important truths about nature and can derive guidance about human conduct. But Machiavelli seems to argue that these are just opinions — what later generations called values — neither better nor worse than any others. One does not have to read *The Prince* too closely, however, to see that Machiavelli goes well beyond this. He is not just putting forward a set of opinions. He is "departing in the greatest possible manner from the orders of others," and doing so, he says, to go after "the effective truth of the matter rather than at its imagination." Here lies the deepest contradiction in Machiavelli's thought.

The Prince's insistent teaching is that those who do not follow its precepts "must" come to ruin. In Chapter XV, Machiavelli is unmistakably clear: the line runs between his precepts, based on how things really are, and precepts based on imagination. In an important sense, then, Machiavelli does not depart from the Christian-classical tradition of basing moral guidance on a nature that exists whether anyone likes it or not.

The revolution, however, is in the fact that Machiavelli does not *discover* the nature from which he draws his precepts. He *manufactures* it before the reader's very eyes. He lists behavioral traits that are "imagined" to be good or bad and finds them inadequate, because they contribute to ruin rather than to success. But what contributes to success? A new list of traits set forth in Chapter XIX, the most important feature of which is that Machiavelli drew it up himself. On this level, Machiavelli is more than a teacher of a list of evils. Rather, somewhat like the serpent in the Garden of Eden, Machiavelli leads modern man to grasp for the power to make his own good and evil for his own sovereign convenience.

Francis Bacon praised Machiavelli for bringing the "stars of the heavens" down into humanity. Like Prometheus (or the Serpent), Machiavelli sought to give man a power that heretofore had belonged to God alone. Much of modern philosophy, following Machiavelli's lead, is founded on the attempt to close mankind's window on the supernatural and to foreclose judgment of human actions by "unrealistic" or "otherworldly" standards. From Descartes through Newton, Hegel, and Heidegger, modern philosophers have built systems. Typically, they begin by setting forth arbitrary premises that channel the entire system in the direction the writer wishes to go. Descartes meant his *Discourse on Method* to build a world that he would know perfectly because he would be its author. Hegel's *Phenomenology of Mind* is written from the perspective of the creator of the universe. The "left-wing Hegelian" Ludwig Feuerbach, who inspired Karl Marx, wrote that man had projected his worthiest qualities onto a god of his own creation, thereby impoverishing himself. Now, says Feuerbach and the Marxist tradition, man must take back his own. The intellectual history of the nineteenth and twentieth centuries is about little other than what the existentialist movement called "heroic" attempts to assert values on the basis of the assertion itself.

The Prince continues to influence our time. Ideas, however, have more than consequences. They have lives of their own. Machiavelli might be surprised at how fully the modern world has adopted his most fundamental teachings. But modern political thought and practice have produced results very different from those at which Machiavelli aimed.

On the level of political thought, the notion that people can create their own values long ago passed from heresy through controversy and into orthodoxy. But whereas Machiavelli manufactured a new moral code for what he considered the most compelling of reasons, the central tenet of modern social science codified by Max Weber says, with a logic more consistent than Machiavelli's, that no reason for valuing anything above anything else is any more reasonable than any other. Indeed, Weber says that value judgments are "demonic," meaning inscrutable. Machiavelli thought that survival, power, and glory were really, demonstrably, the highest human things — at least if we don't consider what might happen after death. Nowadays, however, those who invent their own values are likely to do it to assert ways of life that Machiavelli would have termed inglorious or even subhuman.

Modern society has absorbed *The Prince*'s teaching about the incompatibility of human interests perhaps more thoroughly than Machiavelli intended. Despite his emphasis on people's natural tendency to sell one another out, despite his insistence that the struggle for leadership necessarily produces more losers than winners, Machiavelli clearly believed that any political community — and, *a fortiori*, any family — would enjoy common advantages if they adjusted their mutual wants and stood by one another. Although, contrary to Aristotle, he did not think man is a political animal, he very much wanted to see political communities. In recent times, however, Western intellectual leaders have carried the notion of incompatible human interests to lengths that Machiavelli would have considered self-destructive and ridiculous. Unlike Machiavelli, Marx and his followers saw nothing but mutual exploitation among buyers and sellers of labor and commodities. They also saw mutual exploitation as the driving force within families. Today it is fashionable to believe that the interests of different races, classes, age groups, and even sexes are inherently incompatible. But, judging by strict Machiavellian standards, societies who think this way must become the rightful prey of others because disunity will render them unable to generate power.

Nowadays, the Machiavellian notion that political arrangements may not be judged by any objective standards of right and wrong, that there is neither any natural nor any divine law, but only the law of will, of success and failure, is almost unchallenged. Even in the United States, whose founding document cites "the laws of nature and nature's God," there is near unanimity among the graduates of the top schools that any mention of natural law is subversive. Positive law is the only law. In European welfare states, as in the Third World or in the communist tradition, law is an act of will, period. But what is the objective of will? The main branch of the Western tradition teaches that the will should learn to conform to natural and divine law. Until about World War II, few in the West argued with the prevailing assumption that power and glory are the proper objectives of statecraft, and that violence is a proper tool. Contemporary Western leaders, however, have lost, along with the scruples of natural and divine law, the very will to kill enemies both foreign and domestic. Machiavelli would hardly have understood why anyone would revolt against divine law and assert absolute sovereignty only to exercise it pusillanimously for petty ends.

Modern states have become far more sovereign than Machiavelli ever thought possible or desirable. During the second half of the twentieth century, modern states have multiplied the size of their bureaucracies while becoming less warlike. They spend roughly half their people's incomes — something that Machiavelli warned against specifically and at length. They enforce laws on everything from walking dogs to raising children. They set curricula for schools and standards for foods. They have eclipsed the churches as founts of authority. They have largely supplanted the functions of parents through day care, and of grown children through social security. Their welfare systems have taken the place of husbands in the lives of countless families. And yet Western European governments feel increasingly unable to send their armed forces in harm's way or even to rid the streets of the drug trade. Nothing could be more foreign to modern states than Machiavellian visions of glory. But note that, like Charles de Gaulle, Machiavelli teaches that states are made by strokes of the sword, that war is the gravedigger of decadence, and that states that cannot generate military power must soon be swept away.

Machiavelli taught the importance of constituting armies and keeping them faithful. In our time as ever, the world's regimes are divided into those that do this well and those that don't. Fidel Castro, Kim-il Sung, and Saddam Hussein — dictators who failed at everything — still managed to maintain their regimes under the worst circumstances by competent attention to military matters. By contrast, Mikhail Gorbachev — whose ministers ordered an assault on dissidents and could find no one to carry it out — may be the ultimate example of how personal incompetence can render useless the greatest concentration of military power in the history of mankind. Modern American leaders, for their part, have given up service in the armed forces: Fewer than half the members of Congress have ever served, and military service is rare among the families of executives, leaders of the media and of academe. Nevertheless, these classes increasingly bemoan the growth within the armed forces of a subculture distinct enough to be contemptuous of the president of the United States. Machiavelli would say that they might as well bemoan the effects of the law of gravity.

The twentieth century was characterized by Mao, Stalin, and Hitler. These paradigms of Machiavelli's irreligious, single-minded founders introduced "new modes and orders" and moved the world on a scale greater even than Rome's. Strictly within Machiavelli's calculus of success and failure, of cruelties well or ill used, each is liable only to the kind of retail criticism Machiavelli leveled against Cesare Borgia. Hitler devoted scarce military resources to the Holocaust, and his maltreatment of occupied Russia and Ukraine was disastrously counterproductive. He overreached and paid the price. Stalin broke whole nations and Mao murderously managed a billion people. But they managed to die in bed. To wonder what kind of sickness afflicted the most willful men of this century as to lead them to murders so monstrously greater than glory, we must step outside what is new, modern, original in Machiavelli. We must seize the bit of classical thought that remains in Machiavelli, namely, that the means of statecraft must bear some proportion to the ends.

The mass slaughters of our century produced very little of anything that Machiavelli, never mind his contemporaries, thought glorious. Recall that in the first book of Plato's *Republic* Socrates convinced Thrasymachus to

reconsider the proposition that right is the interest of the stronger by showing him that all-powerful dictators waste their strength and even hurt themselves unless they know the difference between what they want and what
they ought to want. Is it possible that the twentieth century's inglorious
carnage might raise in Machiavelli's mind the possibility that right is not
the interest of the stronger? That any desire, any idea, that leads to Ausch-
witz or the Gulag is inherently inglorious and must be objectively wrong?
And if these things are objectively wrong, what is objectively right, and
why? Of course, by beginning to think this way, any Machiavellian would
be switching sides in our civilization's central quarrel.

But note: The enormities committed by this century's monsters are all
too proportional to the millennial ends of national socialism and marxism.
To evaluate the *ends* of statecraft, we must look for help from Plato's side of
the quarrel, not Machiavelli's.

The Prince is a great book. The purpose of this Introduction, as well as
of the comments that follow the text, is to urge the reader to read it slowly,
on all its levels. Machiavelli is a playful writer. Any reader who habitually
plays with this master will be more than ready to deal with run-of-the-mill
minds.

Words and Power

ANGELO M. CODEVILLA

Traduttore traditore: Translator, traitor. So goes an old Italian saying. Machiavelli offers the translator more than the normal incentives to translingual treason. He writes with apparent disregard for grammar and uses the same unspecialized words to convey different meanings in different contexts. His text is full of puns. He writes the way baseball's Casey Stengel used to speak. The translator is tempted at every turn to "clean up" the text and to specify ambiguous meaning. But he cannot do so without impressing his own interpretation upon the text.

Machiavelli, for instance, uses the verb *convenire* and the adjective *conveniente* in diverse contexts to refer to things as different as pertinence, rightfulness, convention, necessity, convenience, or expediency. Clearly, it matters greatly whether he judges an action rightful or expedient. But his art largely consists of his ability to change the meaning of words. This allows him to use both the denotation and the various connotations of words for his own rhetorical purposes. Thus, in some contexts he fuses the concepts of rightfulness, expediency, and convention, while in others he intends only one. Similarly, the word *stato* can and does mean personal status, the nation, or political condition, while *ordine* can mean an orderly state of things, a command, a regime, or a way of organizing things.

If the translator chooses among the meanings of Machiavelli's words, he implicitly alters the nature of the relationship that Machiavelli intended to establish with his readers. Consider the Epistle Dedicatory. The author of one of the better-known contemporary translations, James B. Atkinson, dedicates his work to his own family by citing Machiavelli's prayer to Lorenzo, that he "take this little gift in the spirit in which I send it."[1] The nature of that spirit, however, is not self-evident. The translation would have it that by his book, Machiavelli wished to have Lorenzo "understand" all that he himself had "understood." But Machiavelli had said he wanted to have Lorenzo *intendere* what he himself had *conosciuto*. The two words imply two very different degrees of intellection. Indeed, *intendere* is often used — albeit colloquially — to indicate deception, as in the common expression *dare da intendere*.[2] Machiavelli could be hinting that he is giving Lorenzo a calculated perception of what he himself had grasped fully.

The differences between Italian and modern English complicate matters still further. Machiavelli's use of second-person pronouns, for example, is anything but univocal. In Italian, Machiavelli often fudges as to whether he is addressing Lorenzo de Medici, whether he is advising all princes (actual or potential), or even whether he is addressing conspirators against princes. So the Italian reader is always encountering signs to be on guard. But the modern English *you* eclipses considerations of number, gender, formality, and informality. Also, Machiavelli makes particularly heavy use of the Italian language's substantial subjunctive component. Since in English the subjunctive is vestigial, many of Machiavelli's sentences imply that something *might* be, whereas corresponding English sentences say that things *are*. Hence, the English reader lacks the means by which to grasp this aspect of Machiavelli's shiftiness.

This is important because the most important questions regarding *The Prince* hinge on Machiavelli's use of words. Does he in fact confuse the adverb *bene* (well) with the noun *bene* (good) so as to collapse the distinction between doing well and doing good? How does Machiavelli change his readers' notion of virtue and goodness? As we shall see, he regards the meaning of such words as wholly plastic. Therefore, he gradually alters their meaning by changing their context. Of course, what Machiavelli means has been debated not only by scholars who lack direct access to Machiavelli's original words but also by Italian speakers. Every translator should therefore balance the need for a smooth text against the need to refrain from injecting a personal interpretation of Machiavelli into the translation.

The present translation of *The Prince* allows scholars and students who do not know Italian to work with a text in which the translator has not resolved the problems of interpretation posed by Machiavelli. To this end I have tried, sometimes at the cost of readability, to translate every word in the same way throughout, while indicating the variant meanings in the endnotes. I have also tried to duplicate Machiavelli's syntax in English with as few changes as possible. Thus, I have tried to render verbs by verbs, nouns by nouns, and so on, and have retained the person, gender, tense, and punctuation of the original, as well as his wide use of the subjunctive mood. As a result, this translation may often appear awkward, but then those who read *The Prince* first in the original are likely to find other translations treacherously smooth. In sum, I content that the sacrifices of elegance made for the sake of faithfulness to the original are justified inasmuch as Machiavelli accomplished his larger ends by artful manipulation of linguistic details.

This translation is based upon the critical edition by Giuseppe Lisio (Florence, 1899), revised by Frederico Chabod, and published in 1968 in a special edition by Giovanni Salerno of Milan.

Machiavelli on Language

Language was Machiavelli's weapon. Whether or not he regarded writing as a surrogate for the political power he could not wield, Machiavelli was a student and practitioner of the power of words. In two of his writings — the *Florentine Histories* and the *Discourse upon Our Language* — he discussed why language is the ultimate weapon.

Aristotle had called language the most characteristically human activity because it is the means by which men do what is peculiarly human: consider which things are better and which worse. Machiavelli agrees that language is the characteristically human tool. But for him this tool serves an end which, though it wholly absorbs man, is not peculiar to human beings. That is, primacy: glory and power over others. A constant theme pervades Machiavelli's writings, that all human action is oriented to this primordial end. Hence Machiavelli's anti-Aristotelian thesis: language is fundamentally a weapon in human struggles. But why the *ultimate* weapon?

In the first book of the *Florentine Histories*, Machiavelli tells us that each of the waves of barbarians that washed over the Roman Empire erased the names of places and institutions it found and substituted its own. Names, he indicates, are nothing but the marks placed on things by those with the power to place them. This brings to mind his discussion of how captured cities ought to be treated, in Chapters III–V of *The Prince*. The contradictory advice he gives rests on a single theoretical point: political power — the power to command the acquiescence of men's minds — depends to some extent on symbols of authority. Where people have obeyed kings out of habit, a conqueror can simply take the title of king. As long as no one from the old ruling family is alive to object, no one else is likely to do so. But where individuals have lived under freely accepted institutions, the mere imposition of new rulers cannot erase each individual's stirring memory of freedom. In Chapter V, Machiavelli seems to suggest that because such memories are ineradicable, one must utterly destroy free cities or risk losing them. Yet destruction of peoples secures possession of places but nothing else. Destruction is not Machiavelli's answer to the question of how to influence men's minds in the face of intellectual opposition. According to Machiavelli, there is a means of conquering men as final as the drawing of the plow over Carthage, but which leaves both men and material intact.[3] That means consists of changing the terms in which people think.

New names preclude the memory of old things. Machiavelli's remark on the conflict of religions applies equally well to intellectual matters, including political ones. He says: "When it happens that the founders of the new religion speak a different language, then the destruction of the old religion is easily effected."[4] Had the Christians not been compelled to express themselves in Latin and Greek, they would have been able to push all that had come before them into permanent oblivion. And, if a language is so structured as to make impossible the articulation of certain thoughts, those thoughts, Machiavelli contends, will be banished forever from the minds of those who speak that language.

Machiavelli formulated the surface of his arguments to please a highly partisan, and not too discriminating, Florentine audience. Dante had claimed to have written his own work on language, *De vulgari eloquentia*, in a language that is *curiale*, courtly. That is, he had tried to describe reality not with reference to this or that community — not even to Machiavelli's Florence — but, rather, in the terms of "the most excellent court of Italy." Dante had written not for any earthly court but for a body whose members "are united by the gracious light of reason." In short, Dante crafted his language to follow the dictates of reason, not of men or of chance. Dante thought language was not to be imposed by power or by convention but to be accepted by reason. Most clearly, Dante did not intend to speak the language of the Roman *Curia*, which was particularistic in both form and content. Indeed, Dante disdained no group so much as the cardinals who made up the pope's *Curia*. Within it, he had written, Christ was bought and sold daily! Yet Machiavelli attacked Dante for speaking the language of the "court of Rome." Machiavelli knew exactly what Dante meant. He disagreed. He believed that language, like every other human tool, serves the interest of some to the detriment of others. But Machiavelli did not argue against Dante. Instead, he baldly accused him of speaking the language of a rival city, of being insufficiently committed to Florence. This did not advance the cause of truth, but it did help Machiavelli prevail with his Florentine audience.

Even with regard to language, Machiavelli's point is that human affairs are about winning and losing. In *The Discourse* he handles Dante in an amusingly rough, even playful, way. But the play is pointed. At the end he claims to have *sgannato* Dante and promises to do the same to all who show insufficient reverence to Florentines. *Sgannare* appears to be a pun. *Ingannare* means "to deceive." *Sgannare* is a rare, contrived way to say "undeceive." That is, Machiavelli claims to have set Dante straight. However, the very common word *scannare* means to kill by bleeding to death. Even Machiavelli's jokes tell us that he plays for keeps.

Machiavelli notes that ultimate political victory does not require the force of arms in every instance. In the midst of his account of how, from the fifth through the eighth centuries, victorious barbarian armies and hordes changed the names of things in the Roman Empire over and over again, Machiavelli underscores the fundamental change that was taking place: barbarians were abandoning the names of their fathers and were taking on the names of Christian saints. While armed men were naming places, the unarmed Christian Church was naming their sons.[5] In fact, Machiavelli points out, by the end of the eighth century, the fiercest of them all, the Longobards, had been so transformed that they retained "only the name" of foreigners.

Language, therefore, is a most powerful weapon in the struggle for primacy, and one peculiarly suited to the unarmed. In the *Discourse upon Our Language*, Machiavelli notes that the most powerful nations of modern Europe — Spain, France, and Germany — "yield" not only to Italy, which did not exist politically, but even to its despised part, Lombardy, for the sake of the language in which Dante, Petrarch, and Boccaccio wrote. The strength of the language makes up for political weakness in a way that will become clear below.

In the *Discourse*, Machiavelli uses Dante as a bad example, against which he sets out his own view of the nature of language, of how languages ought to be judged, and of how they interact. He *uses* Dante. Although Machiavelli aims his fundamental criticism at the substance of Dante's position, on the surface he does little but attack a caricature of Dante.

For Dante, the function of language is to describe the nature of things. To the extent that men understand the place of everything in a divinely ordered natural hierarchy, they may attune themselves to reality. Words express men's best understanding of how every piece of reality fits with every other. Therefore, although words are not quite the means of grace, they have much to do with steering men toward saving truth or damning error. Consequently, ways of speech may be impartially judged, as well as improved, by addition and deletion. No expression is truly foreign if it aptly describes something.

Machiavelli fights Dante's view of language with arguments that embody his own. He claims to make his case not with "general words and conjectures" but with "lively reasons." His thesis is that languages are essentially particular articulations of the universal struggle for primacy. No

language can be *curiale*. Each can express only the particular tastes, preferences, and interests of its maker. All speech thus is a form of rhetoric. It
may be necessary to point out that Machiavelli refers not just to languages
like Latin and Spanish but primarily to modes of speech, kinds of discourse,
approaches to argument. He advances his thesis by means of appeals —
sometimes gross ones — to the pride and *amor proprio* of the Florentine
people. The things that words express are of little importance next to the
success words have in moving the audience in the desired direction. The
point is not to describe but to gain the support of one's audience.

For Machiavelli, the best language is the one *più in prezzo*, the one most
appreciated or, in modern jargon, the most operative. Every language is
somebody's tool. Each is the result of struggle and accident. The difference
between a better and a worse manner of speaking is the degree of success
each achieves. A language is not better for being the exclusive bearer of a
new art or concept. Its particular aptitude just gives it a better position
against its competitors. Competition is the only test of worth. Florentine
writers were able to achieve great success because their language happened
to be most apt for expressing the kind of poetry most prized in the thirteenth
century. The best verbal flag is the one most saluted. Dante's language was
highly regarded. But Dante was most irksome to Machiavelli, because he
succeeded in putting his mark on one of the world's great languages without
thereby intending to advance the cause of his city, his country, or himself.
He was a great creator who missed true greatness because he did not have
the right outlook on what he was doing. Machiavelli blames Dante's *dot-
trina*, that is, Christianity, for the waste of such enormous talent.

Machiavelli believed Dante was blind to the main fact of life: struggle.
Indeed, Machiavelli draws a parallel between the life of language and the
life of politics. Like people, languages are shaped largely by contacts with
their neighbors. Each party uses and is used by the other. Like nations,
languages build themselves up by taking in foreign elements. But the important question for Machiavelli is which languages, which nations, which
orders, succeed in using others piece by piece as building blocks for their
own edifice and which give themselves up little by little by adopting the
structure of others. Some ways of speaking "disorder," while others "are
disordered."

Rome was great because its armies consisted of two hundred thousand
foreigners and a mere twelve thousand Romans. "Nonetheless," says Machiavelli, "because the [latter], with their chiefs, were the nerve of the army,
because they all served under the Roman discipline and order, those armies
kept the Roman name, authority, and dignity." But Rome was able to man-

age subject forces many times the size of its own only as long as its forces were united by the purpose of conquest. Machiavelli blames Dante for having used twenty Florentine legions in his writings, and yet denying Florence its due. This is the essence of the *Discourse*.

The implications of the *Discourse* for Machiavelli's other writings are clear. Machiavelli will use a wide variety of modes in his writings. He may even bring into his treatises the words of men unfriendly to his ends. There will appear to be confusion and contradiction. But because Machiavelli is the purposeful master of his art, all the conflicting modes of speech will be serving one only — his own. The reader should look for Machiavelli's legions to "disorder" far larger ones and get them to fight on his side.

Strategic Use of Language in *The Prince*

The Prince is remarkable not because it tells tales of perfidy and gore, not even because it speaks well of tyranny, but because it thoroughly changes the terms of political discourse. Machiavelli's contemporaries objected to *The Prince* not as virgins shocked by political horrors they did not know existed but because the book presents evil as if it were neither evil nor good but merely useful or counterproductive. By the end unwary readers find themselves agreeing that both good and evil have their worthy places in a new ethical framework structured by the concepts of necessity and usefulness.

Because the strong and wily inevitably dominate the weak and unwary, it is useful to know how to dominate. But why should anyone want to dominate? What is the use of it? Who needs it, and why? Machiavelli does not address such questions explicitly. As we have seen, he considers explicit argument less effective in moving men than other means — and, of course, he believes that moving men is the prime objective of speech. He fundamentally believes that men are moved not by their abstract perceptions of good and evil but by the "lively reasons" of their appetites and fears. Passions are what is truest about men. Human life takes place essentially on this level.

Thoughts, therefore, cannot be judged in terms of good and evil, that is, in terms of other thoughts, but must be measured by how effectively they stir up desires and fears that result in successful, self-serving action. Thoughts that hinder such action must be suppressed, lest they result in defeat and death for those who think them. But, paradoxically, thoughts may not be combated by actions alone. They are vulnerable only to their own kind. They can be vanquished only by opponents that can infiltrate their camp.

Self-consciously polemic thoughts, if smuggled in among unsuspecting thoughts, will defeat them every time. In short, Machiavelli believes that all writing is inherently polemical. His own writing, as a consequence, is self-consciously polemical.

An example of this is the manner in which Machiavelli treats God's will regarding political matters. In Chapter VI, he begins to define the source of political virtue, the meaning of goodness in politics, by citing "Moses, Cyrus, Romulus, Theseus, *and similar ones*" (emphasis mine). After saying that one must not discuss Moses because he was "a mere executor of the things that were ordered to him by God," he assures the reader that the actions of the others are not different from those of Moses, "who had such a great tutor."[6] He stresses this lest we miss the point that God himself ordained the things that the others did. But Machiavelli gives no details of what Cyrus, Romulus, and Theseus did. A few pages later, however, at the end of Chapter VI, he mentions an individual who, he says, "well [*bene*] will have some connection with those others,"[7] so much so that "I want that he suffice me for *all similar ones*" (emphasis added). The individual was Hiero of Syracuse. Thus does Machiavelli make Hiero, one of the ancient world's bloodiest tyrants, the paradigm for the group of great founders, including Moses, and therefore for God himself. This cannot properly be called an argument in favor of Hiero's kind of politics. It is an act designed to remove the stigma of ungodliness from a kind of political morality.

A similar act takes place in Chapter XIII. Immediately after recounting Hiero's bloodiest deed, Machiavelli says that David — who, as everyone then knew, was God's chosen instrument — like Hiero, preferred his own arms to those of others. Once again the translator must follow the text closely and say that, with Saul's arms, David could not "well avail himself of himself." If, however, the translator merely says, with Atkinson, that David could not fight well in Saul's armor, the reader will miss Machiavelli's point that, regardless of theologians' arguments, the cardinal, yea, even the divine rule of politics is to avail one's self of one's self for one's own purposes.

Machiavelli is the first philosopher to espouse the techniques, as well as some of the ends, we now associate with advertising. The importance of his work lies more in the mental habits it inculcates than in the demonstrative propositions it advances. His work, especially *The Prince*, is filled with tales of gore and treachery. To what end? Everyone knew such things happened. Why did Machiavelli insist on mentioning them so frequently and in such detail? He never made a proper argument about the good or evil of these things — though the meaning of good and evil is perhaps the central question of *The Prince*. Machiavelli should not even be accused of saying that bloody dishonesty is always the best policy, given his revelation that force and fraud lead as often to disaster as to success. Then why so much blood and treachery? The answer becomes clear when we remember that Machiavelli did not mean to argue as much as he meant to act. The vivid portrayal of political defeat is a fearsome thing. Machiavelli never argues explicitly that earthly suffering and death are the worst fates; he just omits any discussion of the possibility that they are not. The only "reason" in which he deals is the conflict between fear and the desire for primacy.[8] The penalty for this sort of unreasonableness is death. Had he argued at length that one ought to worry less about the life of the soul and more about the death of the body, he would not have succeeded as well as he did in pressing these very themes upon his readers by uncontradicted lively images.

The Prince is about the advancement of such themes. It is not a collection of political recipes — most of which are inconsistent. Rather, the politically pornographic recipes serve to reorient political morality. The classical-Christian authors whom Machiavelli was consciously renouncing (Chap. XV) had said that acts might be more or less good or evil in themselves and in the intentions of those who perform them. They may, however, have consequences entirely unrelated to their character or to the intentions of their doers. But because no one can know the consequences of any act, its goodness still depends on the above two factors. Machiavelli, however, mentions nothing about the inherent worth of actions. As for intentions, he assumes that men are more or less intelligent but equally selfish. He writes as if the only knowledge we can have is of consequences. Anyone who accepts these tacit arguments will not look beyond his discussion of which political acts may lead to success in establishing and maintaining political primacy. Given this end, good is sometimes evil, and evil sometimes good. After discussing awhile in such terms, the reader acquires new mental habits. To the extent that language and the moral order it expresses are conventional, as Machiavelli insists, he has succeeded in changing political reality.

Still, Machiavelli does present answers to philosophical questions, albeit implicitly. Francis Bacon's observation, "We are much beholden to Machiavelli and others that wrote what men do, and not what they ought to do" is misleading. Men do, and always have done, all sorts of things. Through philosophy men seek to discover which among the things they do are better and more worthy of being done, and which are worse. All but the most mindless reporting of human affairs rests upon philosophical judgment. Nevertheless, Bacon's statements and similar ones are proof of Machiavelli's triumph. He did not cut the tie that has bound *is* and *ought* since the pre-Socratic physicists. Rather, he manipulated the words that express what *is* in a way that implies an *ought* cut to Machiavellian specifications. Moreover, Bacon's statement applies not to Machiavelli but to latter-day positivists whose political theory consists of identifying statistically significant behavior. But Machiavelli is anything but a pollster or a market researcher. Clearly, he claims to describe behavior that is not average, nor even exemplary of the average, but simply exemplary.

I now offer an example of Machiavelli's verbal warfare in the cause of a new morality. I will suggest that his mode of war becomes visible only when the text is closely followed.

Virtue, Doing Well, and Doing Good

Can anything be bad that leads one to prevail over other men? Can anything be good that leads one to succumb? These issues are the spinal column of *The Prince*'s skeleton. It is generally agreed today that the Italian word *virtù*, following the Latin *virtus*, always meant not virtue but power. This is wrong. The significance of *virtus* derived directly from the Platonic-Aristotelian concept of specific use. Thus the virtue of a physician qua physician is different from that of a warrior qua warrior. The difference between the virtue of a horse and of a man follows directly from the different activities peculiar to horses and men. A man of *virtus* is strong in the qualities proper to a man. Both Plato and Aristotle wrote of the peculiar qualities that the political art required. Although it is true that the Roman notion of virtue was more circumscribed by the horizons of the city, neither Livy nor Cicero nor Tacitus was the first to equate virtue and mere power. It was Machiavelli himself.

The fundamental distinction in *The Prince* is that one succeeds either because of virtue or because of fortune. Machiavelli thoroughly explains his views on fortune in Chapter XXV. The bulk of the book, Chapters III–XXIV, is about the meaning of virtue. At the beginning of Chapter VIII he seems to introduce factors other than virtue that make for success: the favor of one's fellow citizens and *scelleratezza*, that is, wretchedness, a combination of cruelty and fraud. Machiavelli claims to have discussed cruelty elsewhere (in the *Discourses*) and declares that he will not discuss the merits of fraud. In doing so, he both protects himself from the potential charge that he should have execrated wretched methods and gives the impression that unresolved questions exist regarding the merit of such methods. The attentive reader soon learns, however, that neither the favor of fellow citizens (in Chap. XVII) nor *scelleratezza* is a category independent of *virtù*. Moreover, as he speaks of virtue and wretchedness in the same breath, he shrinks the moral distance between them.

In the second paragraph of Chapter VIII, Machiavelli first cites the example of the Sicilian tyrant Agathocles, who, from humble origins, raised himself to power, and who always led a *vita scellerata*. But, says Machiavelli, "he accompanied his wretchedness with such virtue of soul and body" that he became successful and secure. What Machiavelli meant by "accompanied" is not clear. Does he mean "matched," as Atkinson would have it? If so, Machiavelli would be saying that Agathocles' virtues of soul and body balanced out and made up for his wretchedness. In other words, virtue and wretchedness are opposites. On the other hand, "accompanied" can mean "accomplish with," in which case Machiavelli would mean that Agathocles did his wretched deeds so virtuously as to achieve the results he did. Taken by itself, the passage can be interpreted either way. I shall show, however, that what follows supports the interpretation that virtue can be a tool for wretchedness. Nonetheless, to understand what Machiavelli is doing, one must not assign to his words meanings more specific than he intends. One must see how ambiguously he departs from classical-Christian morality at first, only to close off any interpretation except the one he intends.

In the following paragraph he writes of Agathocles as if the only possible sources of success were virtue and fortune. The word *scelleratezza* does not reappear. He begins by flatly stating that Agathocles' rise was not due to fortune, or at most only a little. He then says that "one can [or may] not yet call [*non si puo ancora chiamare*] virtue to kill one's own citizens, to be without faith, without pity, without religion." How differently Atkinson renders matters just by changing the order of Machiavelli's words: "yet it cannot be termed." Does Machiavelli mean, as Atkinson would have him, that to call Agathocles' successful actions virtuous would be untruthful and that one cannot, therefore, call them virtuous? Or, on the other hand, does Machiavelli's location of *ancora* suggest that people, being so backward, would not accept calling what Agathocles did virtuous, and therefore one *may not yet* call such things by the names they deserve? At this point, good arguments can be made for either interpretation. There is no doubt, however, that through such double meanings Machiavelli is preparing his readers to accept radical ideas. It is also clear again that in order to decide what Machiavelli means, one must be sure of what he says.

Immediately after the passages cited above, Machiavelli says that Agathocles' methods can gain one empire but not glory. But does lack of glory mean that the methods are naturally loathsome or that the people who do the glorifying are prudish and unenlightened, or a bit of both? In the following sentence he says two things: If one were to consider Agathocles' virtue" in the things he did, there would be no reason to judge him below the most excellent leaders. Nonetheless, his cruelty, inhumanity, and so forth "do not consent that he be celebrated among the most excellent men." Clearly, Machiavelli says that insofar as virtue is concerned, Agathocles does not rank below the most excellent, that this bloody tyrant was at least as virtuous as anyone who ever lived, but that his cruelty and so forth *do not consent that he be celebrated.* In other words, men will not permit Agathocles' rightful celebration because they have aversions to *scelleratezza.*

The final sentence of this paragraph, however, seems to contradict this line of argument by apparently recalling the distinction among virtue, fortune, and "other" factors leading to success (significantly, he does not name any). But in fact this sentence takes back nothing. Of course, says Machiavelli, one cannot attribute to virtue or fortune what Agathocles achieved without either. But by saying that fortune played no part in his success and that Agathocles was a virtuous man, he implies that *scelleratezza* is part of virtue. But one may not yet say it.

Once people get used to things, avowing them becomes easier. There follows a discussion of a less successful bloody traitor, in which, as in the rest of *The Prince,* Machiavelli mentions no factors that make for success except virtue and fortune. Oliverotto de Fermo won power by betraying and murdering his stepfather but lost both power and life when he fell into a trap similar to the one he had set for his stepfather. Oliverotto was outdone at his own game by that paragon of Machiavellian virtue, Cesare Borgia. What was wrong with Oliverotto? Did he receive the just wages for his misdeeds, or did he suffer because of inferior technique?

Machiavelli answers by asking the reader how Agathocles, "after infinite betrayals and cruelties," could live peacefully in his city even in time of war while other cruel men succumbed even in time of peace. His answer: cruelties can be used *male* or *bene.*

Now, both of these words can be either adverbs or nouns, the first meaning "ill" or "evil," the second "well" or "good." Here, as regards cruelties, the use is clearly adverbial. The notion that something good can be put to ill use and that something evil can be put to good use is certainly not foreign to classical and Christian philosophy. But then Machiavelli continues: "Well used can be called those" and here he inserts a parenthesis "if of evil [*male*] it is licit to say well [*bene*]." He had been speaking of cruelties *well* or *ill* used. By using *male* as a noun, he suggests that evil itself may be praiseworthy, which is different. To consider this is to confuse the concepts of evil and good. Philosophically that is possible only on the basis of a concept superordinate to both. But in classical thought, nothing is higher than the good save its Divine Author. Here Machiavelli is touching the most important of matters.

One can see no hint of this in Atkinson's translation: "the good or bad use of ruthless measures. Such use can be termed 'good' — if it is suitable to use the word 'good' of things that are evil." Used instead of "licit," the word "suitable" hides the fact that here Machiavelli is worried not about whether it is right or proper to speak *bene* or *male* but about whether his audience will accept the proposition. "Suitable" connotes nature; "licit" connotes convention. The careless reader will miss the fact that Machiavelli is ready to call evil good to the extent that it is licit, socially permissible, to say well of evil.

But let us return to the text. Those cruelties are well used that assure one's political primacy. Badly used are those cruelties that have no "end." Those who commit purposeful atrocities, like Agathocles, "can have some remedy for their *stato* with God and man." Those who do otherwise must perish. As Machiavelli has moved closer to taking control of the language of the discussion, the grounds on which one could argue that Agathocles was not virtuous have shrunk.

Up to Chapter XV, Machiavelli had cast doubt upon the then-accepted meaning of virtue and had begun to train his reader, as it were, to use "virtue," "good," and "evil" in a new way. In Chapters XV through XIX, he completes his mastery of these words. Moreover, in doing so he leaves no doubt that he is not just affirming one set of opinions over and against another, but that he is conquering error with truth. At the outset of Chapter XV he states that, especially in the discussion about to follow, he will depart from the orders of others. But he promises to go straight to the "effective truth of the thing" rather than "to its imagination," because he wishes "to be useful" to him who perceives what he is saying. Note in passing his tacit claim that "the others" who had argued virtue is the right order of the soul were not useful and that only what contributes to primacy is useful. The paramount place of primacy in the hierarchy of personal goals is already beyond question. The key point here is his opposition of "effective truth" and "imagination." Effective truth presumably differs from any other kind in that it is able to "effect" itself. Anything else, he emphasizes below, is not *vero*, not true.

Again he sets up a dichotomy: in the realm of practice, the opposite poles are "how one lives" and "how one ought to live." But he equates how one ought to live with the "imagination of things," that is, with futility and untruth. In the next phrase he points out that because of the way things are, he who lives as one ought finds ruin rather than preservation. One does not have to ask how compelling is an "ought" that is based on untruth, on disregard for the way things really are, and that leads one to ruin. One reflexively rejects it and just as reflexively leans toward Machiavelli's effective truth.

The truly compelling feature of the true world, says Machiavelli, the feature that makes it dangerous to live by imagination, is the prevalence of people who are "not good." But by now the inquiring mind has been led to ask, "Not good according to what standard?" Certainly by the "effective" standards of what is "true," the denizens of the world live quite properly, although the classical-Christian standard of truth and goodness has been disqualified.

Having thus prepared his reader, Machiavelli says that a prince who wants to maintain himself (by now the reader has been trained to agree that this is the paramount good) "must learn to be able to be not good,[9] and to use it and not to use it according to necessity." Throughout the first fifteen chapters, the maintenance or the improvement of one's position has tacitly acquired greater and greater importance, as Machiavelli has increasingly undermined the classical-Christian standard of how one ought to live. *Now he explicitly recognizes the desire for personal primacy as "necessity," something so important that "good" and "not good" must serve it.*

The rest of the brief chapter consists of two interwoven lists of the personal traits that most men praise or blame. After Machiavelli has laid them out, he says that everyone would like to be thought of as possessing the traits "held to be good." In other words these traits are prized by "imagination." In "truth," they are not praiseworthy, blameworthy, or even noteworthy for their own sake but only because they are prized by the many *who do not live according to the truth.* Machiavelli never answers directly whether or not one should have the qualities that are "held good." Instead he notes the (true but irrelevant) fact that to have them all is impossible, only to conclude that one ought to flee the infamy of the vices that would cause him to lose *lo stato.* Thus Machiavelli leads the reader to focus not on the qualities themselves but on their infamy — and above all on the central question: What will help or hurt my gaining *lo stato*? Then, lest there be doubt, he tells the reader not to worry about the infamy of the vices that would help him gain or keep *lo stato.*

In short, he identifies the set of traits held blameworthy with vices and, implicitly, the opposite list with virtue. But then, lest any attentive reader be left behind, he says that if one will well consider everything, one will find some seemingly virtuous things that lead one to ruin, and other seemingly vicious things that lead to one's well-being. Thus — *and this is the book's center of gravity* — from the sovereign standpoint of *bene essere* (well-being), established in its sovereign place by the means we have seen, Machiavelli argues that what is imagined to be virtue is not necessarily good and what is imagined to be vice is not necessarily bad. One may notice here a summary inversion of Plato's principal thesis in Book I of the *Republic* and in *Gorgias*, to wit: what leads one to power and riches is not necessarily good or virtuous. For Machiavelli the path to power and riches is the very definition of goodness.

Let us look at both sets of these imagined qualities:

Imagined Virtue or Goodness	Imagined Vice or Evil
liberality	*miserliness*
giving	*rapaciousness*
pity	*cruelty*
faithfulness	*fickleness*
effeminacy-pusillanimity	*ferocity and spiritedness*
humaneness	*haughtiness*
chastity	*lasciviousness*
simplicity (gullibility)	*astuteness*
softness	*hardness*
superficiality	*gravity*
religion	*unbelief*

The reader should be struck by the obvious artificiality of the contrasts. Neither Aristotle, Plato, or St. Thomas Aquinas would have counted gullibility and pusillanimity among the components of virtue. Nor would any of them have held that a man ought invariably to be moved by the qualities Machiavelli says are imagined good, while shunning all the qualities Machiavelli says are imagined to be bad. Clearly, the lists are straw men erected to be knocked down. To discredit a conception of good and evil founded upon these two lists is easy. The point of the exercise is to make impossible any reference to objective standards of good and evil. Henceforth good and evil will be small stuff in the new order.

Machiavelli begins the demolition in Chapter XVI by a bit of common sense about money and politics, parts of which could well have been written by Plato, Aristotle, or St. Thomas. He argues that a government's "liberality," which generally enjoys a better reputation than miserliness, may well lead to the impoverishment of the citizenry, as well as to the discredit and ruin of that government. When a government tries to earn for itself the goodwill of the citizenry by giving it gifts, the government is compelled to be "taxy." But although a government can never satisfy those to whom it gives, it will always be hated and opposed by those from whom it takes. In the end, a government that impoverishes all for the benefit of some will have certain enemies and uncertain friends. The theoretical point is simple and irrefutable: the quality of liberality is good only in relation to the ends it may reasonably be expected to attain. The policy recommendation is fiscal prudence. The practical maxim that Machiavelli draws from it — be generous only with your enemies' money — is somewhat more disputable. But on the whole Chapter XVI is a pause between two waves of radical assault.

Chapter XVII begins in the same vein: by being less than cruel one day, a ruler might bring about immeasurable cruelties the next. Therefore, on any given occasion a cruel act might turn out to be merciful. Yet, just when it seems Machiavelli means only to go down the list of the contrasts he has established in order to produce a set of prudential caveats, he goes abruptly to the heart of the matter.

How does one, he asks, gain the steadfast allegiance of men, by love or by fear? He quickly changes the terms of the question by asking whether one wins men by "price" or by "greatness of spirit." His answer is that it is better to be feared, because people may easily set aside the bonds of love for their own profit, whereas "dread is held fast by a fear of pain which never abandons you." But Machiavelli does not make as much of this insight as Hobbes does later. He immediately adds the qualification that fear must be instilled in such a way as not to breed hatred even stronger than itself.[10] Thus far, the point he has made with respect to cruelty (the goodness of its use depends on circumstances) is not much weightier than the one he made with regard to miserliness. But having raised a radical point and retreated, he comes back immediately to clinch it.

Machiavelli then considers the circumstance of armies. As we have seen elsewhere (notably in Chapters XII–XIV), armed forces are prototypical of political relationships. He offers the example of Hannibal, who led armies composed of different peoples into foreign lands and overcame the primordial political problem of getting people with conflicting interests to suffer and sacrifice for a common cause. He did it, says Machiavelli, by his "inhuman cruelty" together with his "infinite virtues." Now, as in the case of Agathocles, one asks what the relationship between inhuman cruelty and virtue is. But whereas in Chapter VIII the answer was merely implied,[11] in Chapter XVII it is clearly stated: "Without [inhuman cruelty], to have this effect, *his other virtues* [*le altre sua virtu*] did not suffice him" (emphasis added). And in the sentence after the next: "And that it be true that his other virtues [*l'altre sua virtu*] would not have sufficed him." Thus Machiavelli makes not just cruelty but *inhuman cruelty* into a virtue and a part of virtue. But Atkinson, like many others, renders *le altre sua virtu* as "the rest of his virtue." This translation only hints at a relationship that Machiavelli now chooses to spell out.

Machiavelli, however, does not wish to overemphasize the role of cruelty. Praise of cruelty is not his main concern. Immediately after making cruelty a virtue, he shows that in republican Rome, Scipio did very well without it. So, from the standpoint of political effectiveness, cruelty is just a tool to be used, sometimes more than others. We are left to conclude that Machiavelli likened cruelty and virtue not so much to exalt the former as to debase the latter.

In Chapter XVIII there is none of the mock fairness of the previous two chapters. Machiavelli does not argue that lies sometimes have more salutary effects than truth. Rather, he discusses whether it is good to tell the truth and keep faith strictly on the basis of what is most helpful in political combat. Tacit elsewhere, the book's fundamental premise — the primacy of conflict and victory in human affairs — becomes explicit. Here it is carried to its logical conclusion.

There are two ways of fighting, says Machiavelli. One way, by means of laws (that is, of the mind) is proper to men; the other, by means of force, is proper to beasts. When the first does not suffice, *conviene* to resort to the second. Therefore, he says, Chiro the Centaur taught ancient princes the ways of both men and beasts. But Machiavelli makes no further mention of ways peculiar to men. Rather, he identifies reason with the fox and force with the lion. Thus he relegates both mental and physical means of struggle to the realm of beasts. At least part of his task is accomplished: he has boldly reduced intelligence to cunning.

Is it virtuous to speak the truth and keep promises? Machiavelli teaches that the real or true standard is: no one should keep a promise when by doing so he would diminish his own power and when the conditions which occasioned the promise are gone. But one must know how to "color" this way of life well and appear faithful and true while being entirely fickle. He chooses but one example: Pope Alexander VI, who, he says, "never did anything, never thought of anything but to deceive men." The very mind of the pope, the very doctrines of the Church, are thus reduced not just to deception but to animal cunning.

Here, then, is the central teaching of *The Prince*: if inhuman cruelty and animal cunning are verified by reality to be necessary to successful human life, then clearly what passes for human virtue in the minds of most people is false. Even more, the common conception of virtue brings defeat and subjugation to *il vulgo*, "the many" who hold it. Thus in the last two paragraphs of Chapter XVIII we see that the common conception of virtue is as a tool to be wielded by the enlightened few who know what is truly important against the unenlightened many, who are ready to sacrifice themselves to abstract notions of goodness.

Machiavelli's *Prince* is not a list of maxims and most certainly not a survey of common behavior. It is an attempt to wholly discredit a certain conception of human virtue. Machiavelli first undermined the concept of virtue by confusing it with murder and fraud. He then filled it with utterly indefensible components and found them wanting. He tried them, however, not according to the standard of classical and Christian philosophers, the standard by which decent families raise their children, but according to his own absolute standard: success in the struggle for primacy. According to that standard, even qualities that had previously been thought proper to animals are shown to be more appropriate to human beings than what Machiavelli has passed off as the common conception of virtue. The qualities that had been counted as good only make those who possess them contemptible. Those which had been thought bad make their possessor hated. But if readers adopt Machiavelli's priorities, they will develop a new list that will make them truly successful and truly virtuous.

The new meaning of virtue arises from the very process that discredited the old. At the beginning of Chapter XIX, in a parody of Aristotle, Machiavelli presents the new components of virtue and vice as a sort of mean between the extremes of the two lists he has discredited in chapters XVI through XVIII. Vice now consists of irresolution, pusillanimity, effeminacy, lightness (superficiality), and indiscriminate rapaciousness — but, pointedly, not rapaciousness toward selected targets. Virtue now seems to consist of strength, gravity (the ability to weigh on things), spiritedness, and greatness. Of course, the new virtue is not the mean between the classical-Christian notion of virtue and the classical-Christian notion of vice. Machiavelli never gave the reader even a peek at classical-Christian ideas of virtue and vice, much less argue against them. Machiavelli's new list is not the "golden mean" of anything. Rather, it represents a new view of what men ought to do to attune themselves to the fundamental truth of the world.

Machiavelli did not argue that what Christian and classical philosophers had thought most important was less so. Rather, he set about fixing new names on the landscape of political morality. Moreover, he did this by the use of lively reasons. That is, he focused readers' attention on the dangers and opportunities in politics, while changing the terms of the discussion. As we have seen, for Machiavelli, words are means of exercising power. *The Prince* was an attack on a political language. Part of Machiavelli's plan of battle was to capture the word *virtue*. He did not destroy virtue; he conquered it. First, he disordered the words of which the concept of virtue consisted, then he reorganized them according to his "new orders" to fight on his side. By doing so, he made it difficult for even the memory of virtue as it was once understood to enter political discourse.

Because it is impossible to understand what Machiavelli says apart from the way in which he says it, one must approach his writings conscious that for him, words are plastic tools subordinated to a rhetorical purpose. But in order even to identify that purpose, one must take into account the questions to which his use of words gives rise.

NOTES

1. *The Prince*, Niccolò Machiavelli, ed. and trans. James B. Atkinson (New York, 1976). Throughout my discussion, I will refer to Atkinson's work as representative of an approach that differs from mine. I do not mean to suggest that Atkinson's translation is the epitome of that approach, but that it represents it as well as any.

2. See the penultimate paragraph of Chap. IX. On the other hand, the expression *intendersene* means specific expertise. Here the meaning is in doubt — except that Machiavelli is making a distinction between Lorenzo's cognition and his own.

3. Language, then, is the timeless equivalent of today's neutron bomb. But it is even more powerful, because it kills only the enemy's inimical *thoughts*.

4. *Discourses* II:5.

5. *Florentine Histories* I. This observation — that the Church had achieved its conquest of the barbarians by the year 800 — differs substantially from Machiavelli's claim in Chap. 13 of *The Prince* that the Church had become powerful by lending its names, and therefore its authority, to rulers beginning with Charlemagne. The Church's fundamental power is its ability to apply the labels "good" and "evil." Even if the pope had never crowned Charlemagne, Machiavellian politics would still have had to confront the Church's fundamental power.

6. The translator must take care here. Atkinson renders the passage

"even though the latter had such a great tutor" because he translates *che* as "even though" instead of "who." In so doing, he blunts a very sharp point. *Prince*, p. 145.

7. Atkinson, however, wholly ignores the word *bene*, which in this context means "and how!" and thereby gives the impression that Hiero of Syracuse is somewhat like the others instead of the paradigm for the whole group. Ibid., p. 151.

8. Thus "it is not reasonable that one who is armed obey one who is unarmed." *Prince* VIII.

9. Atkinson translates this as "must learn *not to be good*" (emphasis mine), i.e., must learn not to be something — to fall short of the acknowledged standard of goodness. In fact, however, Machiavelli says one must learn *to be not good*, i.e., to adhere to quite a different standard.

10. Machiavelli contends that as long as men have seen that a leader is willing to kill, but have not themselves been hurt by him and do not feel immediately threatened in their persons or goods, they will not place themselves in jeopardy for the sake of other potential victims.

11. Wretchedness accompanied virtue, or wretchedness virtuously done.

The Prince

[Epistle Dedicatory]
Nicolaus Maclavellus ad Magnificum Laurentium Medicem
(Niccolò Machiavelli to the Magnificent Lorenzo dei Medici)

Most of the time, those who desire to acquire favor with a prince are accustomed[1] to approaching him with those among their things which they hold most dear, or which they see him take pleasure in, which is why one often sees horses, arms, cloths of gold, precious stones, and similar ornaments worthy of their greatness being presented to them. Therefore, I, desiring to offer myself to your magnificence with some testimony of my services to it,[2] have not found among the goods of my house anything that I hold dearer or that I esteem as much as the understanding of the actions of great men, learned by long experience with modern things and by continuous reading of ancient ones which I, having thought out at length and examined with great diligence and now reduced to a small volume, send to your Magnificence. And, even though I judge this work unworthy of the latter's presence, *tamen*[3] I trust enough that it must be acceptable to it because of its[4] humaneness, considering that no greater gift could be made

1. The verb *sogliono* (third pers. pl., act.) is usually translated as an adverb, e.g., "commonly," "customarily." Sometimes it is even rendered as "it is customary." Modern Spanish and Italian have words related to it, but not English. The word is related both to the Latin *solium*, which means throne or seat of power, and to *solito*, usual. It conveys the sense of an ingrained habit, and a proper one at that. The closest English word is "wont."

2. *Questa*, referring directly to Lorenzo's Magnificence, and only indirectly to Lorenzo. Although Lorenzo may confuse his Magnificence with himself, Machiavelli does not.

3. Nevertheless (Lat.). Machiavelli's use of words and phrases in Latin, the language of the Church, of authority and solemnity, is not casual. The reader should ask why, at any given point in the work, Machiavelli chooses to endow an example, a noun, an adjective, or a mere conjunction with the aura of Latin.

4. *Sua* refers to magnificence (feminine in Italian) and — indirectly — to Lorenzo de'Medici. Humaneness was frequently used to indicate courteous goodness.

to it than to give it[5] the possibility of being able to perceive[6] in a very short time all that I have come to know in many years and with many personal discomforts and dangers. Which work I have neither adorned nor filled with expansive expressions, or with pompous and magnificent words, or with whatever other allurement or extrinsic ornamentation with which many are used to describe and adorn their things; because I have wanted either that no thing honor it, or that the nature of the treatment and the weight of the subject matter alone make it acceptable. Nor do I want that it be reputed a presumption if a man of low and base estate dares to discuss and judge the government of princes, because, just as those who draw countrysides place themselves low in the plains to consider the mountains and high places, and they place themselves high upon mountains to consider the low ones, similarly, to know well the nature of peoples one needs to be a prince, and to know well that of princes one needs to be of the people.

Let your magnificence therefore take this little gift in the spirit in which I send it; which, if it be diligently considered and read by it,[7] it will know therein an extreme desire of mine, that it[8] might come to that greatness which fortune and your other qualities promise. And, if your magnificence from the apex of your height sometime will direct the eyes to these low places, it will know how undeservedly I bear a great and continuing malignity of fortune.

5. Machiavelli writes the impersonal pronoun *li* rather than the personal pronoun *le*. *Li* can refer to magnificence or to Lorenzo. Had he used *le*, the reference would have been unambiguously to Lorenzo. Machiavelli is a master of purposeful imprecision.

6. *Intendere*, which is what Machiavelli offers to Lorenzo and what I translate as "to perceive," implies a less complete grasp of the subject than *conoscere*, "to know," which Machiavelli claims to have done himself. Note, for example, the common expression *dare da intendere*, which means to "pass off" or "to fool." On the other side of the argument, note that the expression *intendersene* means to be well practiced in a discipline. Here, context argues for the former interpretation.

7. I.e., by that magnificence.

8. I.e., that same magnificence.

I

Quot sint principatuum et quibus modis sint acquirantur
(Of how many kinds are principalities, and in what ways they are acquired)

All the states[9] and all the dominions which have had and have lordship[10] over men have been and are either republics or principalities. And the principalities are either hereditary, where the bloodline of their lord have been princes for a long time, or they are new. And the new ones either are all new, as Milan was to Francesco Sforza,[11] or they are like members added to the hereditary estate of the prince who acquires them, as is the kingdom of Naples to the king of Spain.[12] These dominions thus acquired are either habituated[13] to live under a prince or used to being free; and they are acquired either with others' arms or with one's own, either by fortune or by virtue.

9. *Stato* means both personal station and state in the modern sense. *The Prince* is about both.

10. *Imperio* here certainly does not mean "empire" as a kind of government, but rather lordship or power.

11. In 1450 Francesco Sforza killed Milan's Ambrosian Republic (Ambrose is Milan's patron saint), which had arisen after the death of Filippo Visconti.

12. Ferdinand the Catholic acquired Naples through the Treaty of Blois in 1504.

13. *Consueti* connotes passivity and rest.

II

De principatibus hereditariis
(Of hereditary principalities)

I will leave aside reasoning of republics, because I reasoned of them at length on another occasion.[14] I will turn only to the principality, and I will go weaving the aforesaid warp, and I will debate how these principalities may be governed and maintained.

I say, then, that there are far smaller difficulties involved in maintaining states hereditary and inured to the bloodline of their prince than in the new ones, because it suffices not to break off the orders of one's ancestors, and then to temporize with accidents: so that, if such a prince is of ordinary industriousness, he will always maintain himself in his state, if there is not an extraordinary and excessive force that deprives him of it; and, though he might become a private man, whatever disaster the occupier might have, he reacquires it.

We have in Italy *in exemplis*[15] the duke of Ferrara, who did not succumb to the attacks of the Venetians in '84, nor to those of Pope Julius in '10, for any other reason than for being in that dominion for ages. Because the natural prince has smaller cause and smaller need to offend: from which it follows[16] that he is likely to be more loved; and, if extraordinary vices do not make him hated, it is reasonable that he be naturally well regarded by his own. And the memories and causes[17] of the innovation are extinguished in antiquity and contrivance of rule: because one change always leaves the indentations for the building of another.

---

14. *Discourses*, Book I.

15. Latin, "for example." The reference is to the Dukes Ercole and Alfonso I d'Este, who fought both the pope and Venice from 1482 to 1513.

16. *Conviene.* The verb *convenire* has meanings which range from custom to convention to appropriate necessity. In philosophical discourse, "convention" is opposed to "nature." Machiavelli's frequent and frequently ambiguous use of the family of words which stem from *convenire* is especially interesting because he sought to reverse the order of importance that the Western philosophical tradition attributes to natural-divine order, and to human will.

17. *Cagioni* here means the causes of resentment, that is, the injuries that, according to Machiavelli, necessarily accompany any political innovation. Habitual acceptance of any order hides the fact that it is built on violence.

III

De principatibus mixtis
(Of mixed principalities)

But the difficulties are in the new principality. And first, if it is not all new, but like an appendage,[18] so that altogether it can be called almost mixed, changes within it spring from a natural difficulty, which is in all new principalities: which is that men willingly change lords believing to improve; and this belief makes them take up arms against him,[19] about which they deceive themselves, because then they see by experience that they have worsened, which follows from another natural and ordinary[20] necessity, which makes it so that one always need offend those whose new prince one becomes, both with men-at-arms and with unnumbered other injuries which the new acquisition pulls along behind itself; so that you[21] have for enemies all those you have offended in occupying that principality, and you cannot keep as friends those who have put you there, being unable to satisfy them in that way which they had presupposed, and being unable to use strong medicines against them, since you are obliged to them; because always, one has need of the provincials' favor in order to enter into a province, though one be most powerful with armies. For these reasons Louis XII of France occupied Milan at once, and at once he lost it;[22] and the first time Ludovico's forces[23] sufficed to take it from him; because the people who had opened doors to him, finding themselves deceived of their opinion and of that future good which they had set before themselves, could not bear the annoyances of the new prince.

It is indeed true that upon acquiring countries that have revolted for the second time, they are lost with more difficulty; because the lord, having

18. *Membro*, a member, a limb, one body politic added to another.

19. Referring to the lord. But in thinking that a new lord will be better, they deceive themselves.

20. *Ordinario*, meaning both "common" and also "pertaining to the order of things."

21. Familiar form, singular.

22. Gained in October 1499, lost in February 1500.

23. Ludovico (il Moro) Sforza took Milan in February 1500. Louis XII retook it in April but lost it in April 1502, after he was defeated by the Holy League of Pope Julius II.

8 Niccolò Machiavelli

taken the occasion of the rebellion, is less respectful[24] as he makes himself secure by punishing offenders, clearing up suspicions, providing for himself in his weakest parts. So that, if to make France lose Milan the first time it sufficed that one Duke Ludovico rumble on the borders, to make it lose [Milan] the second time it was necessary to have the whole world against him, and his armies extinguished or chased out of Italy; which sprang from the above-mentioned causes. Nonetheless, it was taken from him both the first and the second time. The general causes of the first have been discussed; it remains now to tell those of the second, and so to see what remedies were available to him, and which someone who might be in his condition can have in order to be able to maintain himself in his acquisition better than France did. I say consequently that these states, which, being acquired, are added onto a state belonging of old to him who acquires, are either of the same province and of the same tongue or they are not. When they be, it is easy to keep them, especially when they are not used to living free; and to possess them securely it suffices to have extinguished the line of the prince who dominated them, because otherwise, if their old conditions are maintained and there is not disparity of customs, men live quietly; as it has been seen that Burgundy, Brittany, Gascony, and Normandy have done, which have been with France for a long time; despite there being disparity of language, nonetheless the customs are similar, and they can mutually carry on among themselves. And whoever acquires them, wanting to keep them, must have two cares: one, that the bloodline of the old prince be extinguished; the other, not to alter either their laws or their taxes; so that in a very brief time it becomes all one body with their old principality.

But when one acquires states in a province of disparate tongues, customs, and orders, here are the difficulties, and here one needs to have great fortune and great industriousness to keep them; and one of the greatest and most lively remedies would be that the person who acquires them might go there to live. This would make the possession more secure and more durable; as did the Turk in Greece;[25] who, [even] with all the other orders observed by him to keep that state, if he had not gone to live there, it was not possible that he keep it. Because, being there, one sees the disorders being born and you can remedy that quickly; [when one is] not living there, one perceives them when they are [already] great and when there is no more

24. The word used is *respetti*, meaning less scrupulous. *Suspetti*, later in the sentence, means both suspects and suspicions.

25. The Turks conquered the Balkan peninsula in 1453 and made Constantinople the capital of their entire empire.

remedy. Beyond this, the province is not despoiled by your officials; the subjects are satisfied with recourse to the prince close by; for which reason, if they want to be good, they have more cause for loving him and, if they want to be otherwise, for fearing him. Whatever foreigner might want to attack that state has greater respect[26] for it, so that, living there, he can lose it with very great difficulty.

The other better remedy is to send colonies into one or two places that may be the fetters to that state;[27] because it is necessary either to do this or to keep enough men-at-arms and infantry there. One does not spend much on colonies and he[28] sends them there without expense to himself, or little, and only offends those from whom he takes the fields and the houses, to give to the new inhabitants, who are a miniscule part of the state[29]; and those whom he offends, remaining dispersed and poor, can never harm him; and all the others remain by one side unharmed, and for this reason should keep quiet, fearful lest they err, for fear that it not happen to them as to those who have been despoiled. I conclude that these colonies do not cost, are more reliable, and offend less; and the offended ones cannot do harm, being poor and dispersed, as is said. By way of which, one has to note that men must either be caressed[30] or extinguished; because they avenge themselves of light offenses, but of the grave ones they cannot. So the offense one does to a man must be such that one not fear vengeance for it.[31] But in keeping men-at-arms there instead of colonies, one spends much more, having to expend all the income of the state on guarding it, so that the acquisition becomes a net loss, and it[32] offends much more, because it does harm to all that state, changing his army by quartering it;[33] the discomfort of which everyone feels, and each one becomes his enemy; and they are enemies who

26. Here "respect" means reticence, and "it" refers to attacking.

27. The literal translation of *compedi* (translated as "key") is "leg irons" or "fetters." The image is of places by whose possession a prince can hold a country in the way that leg irons hold a man.

28. I.e., the prince does not spend much on colonies. The prince sends them out with little expense to himself.

29. Referring to those whose fields and houses were taken.

30. Another connotation of *vezzeggiare* is "to humor." The contemporary political term "stroking" captures the essence of it.

31. Cf. *Discourses* III:6: "He who is dead cannot think of vengeance."

32. "It" refers to relying on men-at-arms instead of colonies.

33. "Tramutando con li allogiamenti el suo esercito" means changing his army (for the worse) by keeping it in quarters, as an occupation force.

can do him harm, [because they] remain in their own homes, though beaten. From all sides, therefore, this [method of] guarding[34] is useless, as that of the colonies is useful.

In a different province he must also, as has been said, make himself chief and defender of the less powerful neighbors, and scheme to weaken the powerful and look out lest by some accident a foreigner as powerful as himself enter there. And it will always happen that he[35] will be put there by those in it who will be malcontent, either because of too much ambition or because of fear; as was earlier seen when the Aetolians put the Romans into Greece; and in every other province they entered, they[36] were put there by the provincials. And the order of things[37] is that when a powerful foreigner enters a province, all the less powerful within it adhere to him, moved by envy against whomever has been placed over them; so much so that he need make no effort at all to gain these lesser powers, because all together immediately lump themselves[38] with the state he has acquired there. He has only to see to it[39] that they not take on too much strength and too much authority; and in order to remain fully the arbiter of that province, he can easily lower those who are powerful with his own forces and with their[40] favor. And whoever will not play this role[41] well, will soon lose that which he will have acquired, and, while he has it, he will have numberless difficulties and annoyances therein.

The Romans played this role[42] well in the provinces they took and sent the colonies, entertained the less powerful without increasing their power, lowered the powerful, and did not allow powerful foreigners to gain a

34. The word is *guardia*, meaning guard. But the context points both to the relative uselessness of the guard troops and to the usefulness of "that" (all the colonies) which have no guard troops but which are themselves something which guard the conquest.

35. Refers to any foreign prince who acquires new territory.

36. The Romans.

37. The natural order of things.

38. The word is *globo*, "globe" ("fanno uno globo col suo stato"), but the meaning is "make common cause" or "jump on the bandwagon."

39. *Pensare*, literally, to think.

40. That is, "the less powerful ones'."

41. Literally, "will not govern this part well." The word *parte* here certainly does not indicate a place, but rather that portion of the art of governing just delineated, and the advice he has given upon it.

42. *Parti* here has the same meaning as in the previous usage.

reputation there. And I want the province of Greece alone to suffice as an example. The Acheans and the Aetolians were entertained by them, the kingdom of the Macedonians was lowered, Antioch was chased out of there; nor did the merits of the Acheans or of the Aetolians ever cause them[43] to permit them[44] to add to any state; nor did the persuasions of Philip ever induce them to be his friend without lowering him; nor could the power of Antioch make them consent to his keeping any state in that province. Because in these cases the Romans did what all wise princes must do, who have to have an eye[45] not only on present disorders but on future ones as well, and have to avoid the latter with all industriousness: because, by providing for oneself beforehand, one can remedy them easily, but if one waits until they draw close, the medicine is not on time, because the illness has become incurable. And of this, it happens as the physicians say of the Etico,[46] which in the beginning of its malignity[47] is easy to cure and difficult to know, but in the progression of time, not having known it at the beginning nor medicated it, it becomes easy to know and difficult to cure. So it happens in the things of state; because, knowing far-off (which is not given except to the prudent) the evils[48] which are borne in it, one quickly cures them, but, not having known them, one allows them to grow so that anyone knows them, there is no longer any remedy for them.

Therefore,[49] the Romans, seeing inconveniences from afar, always remedied them and never let them go on in order to run from a war, because they knew that one does not escape war, but one defers it to the advantage of others; therefore, they wanted to make war on Philip and Antioch in Greece, in order not to have to do it in Italy; and they could have avoided both for a while, which they did not choose to do. Nor did that which is all day long in the mouths of the wise of our times ever please them, namely, to enjoy the

43. The Romans.

44. The Romans sought the alliance of the Aetolian League against Philip of Macedon and the Achean League. After these powers were defeated in 197 B.C., the Romans turned on their allies and defeated them in 190 B.C.

45. *Riguardo*, i.e., have to keep an eye out for.

46. This word has two entirely different meanings. The indicated one is a consumptive disease, usually translated "Aetolian fever." The other is "ethics." A pun would hardly be out of character.

47. *Male* means illness, as well as evil and bad.

48. *Mali*, evils or illnesses.

49. In the sixteenth century *però*, "however," also meant *perciò*, "therefore."

fruits[50] of time, but rather those[51] of their virtue and prudence; because time pushes everything before it and can bring with it good as well as evil, and evil as well as good.

But let us return to France and examine whether it has done any of the things said; and I will speak of Louis and not of Charles, whose proceedings have been better seen because he has held possessions in Italy longer; and you[52] will see how he did the contrary of those things which must be done in order to keep a differently constituted state.

King Louis was put into Italy by the ambition of the Venetians, who wanted to earn for themselves half the state of Lombardy by his coming. I do not want to blame the part[53] taken by the king; because, wanting to begin to put one foot into Italy and not having friends in this province — on the contrary, all doors being closed to him by the behavior of King Charles[54] — he was forced to take what friendships he could: and his venture would have succeeded had he made no errors at all in the other maneuvers. Having conquered Lombardy, the king instantly re-earned the reputation Charles had taken from him: Genoa yielded; Florentines became his friends; marquis of Mantova, duke of Ferrara, Bentivogli, madonna of Forli, lord of Faenza, of Pesaro, of Rimini, of Camerino, of Piombino, Luccans, Pisans, Sienese, all approached him to be his friend. And then the Venetians were able to consider the temerity of the choice[55] they had made; they who, to acquire two pieces of land in Lombardy, had made the king lord of two-thirds of Italy.

Let one now consider with how little difficulty the king could have kept his reputation in Italy if he had observed the aforesaid rules and kept all those friends of his secure and defended, who were always in need of staying with him, being numerous and weak, some fearful of the Church and others of the Venetians, and by means of them he could easily have assured himself of whoever remained great there. But he was no sooner in Milan

50. *Beneficio* means literally "blessings" or "profit."

51. Referring to "blessings."

52. Plural.

53. That is, the king's strategy vis-à-vis Venice. Louis XII promised Venice the city of Cremona and the valley of the Adda River in exchange for Venice's help.

54. In 1495, Charles VIII had been fought by a coalition of Venice, Milan, Florence, Naples, Mantua, Spain, and the Holy Roman Empire.

55. *Partito*, literally, "party," can mean side, choice, opinion, and even enterprise or quarrel. It is rendered as *decision* in the next paragraph. ("Nor did he realize that with this decision . . . .")

than he did the contrary, giving aid to Pope Alexander so that he might occupy Romagna. Nor did he realize that with this decision he was making himself weak, taking from himself friends and those who had thrown themselves on his lap, and making the Church great, adding so much that is temporal to the spiritual which already gives it so much authority. And, first having made one error, he was constrained to keep on doing such until, he was forced to come into Italy to put an end to the ambition of Alexander, to prevent him from becoming lord of Tuscany. It did not suffice him to have made the Church great and to have taken his friends from himself so that,[56] since he wanted the Kingdom of Naples, he divided it with the king of Spain; and whereas he had been earlier, the arbiter of Italy, he put a partner there, so that the ambitious of that province and those unhappy with him might have a recourse; and whereas he could have left in that kingdom a king who was his own client, he took such a one out in order to put in one [king] who might chase him from it.[57]

To desire to acquire is truly something very natural and ordinary, and always, when men do it who can, they will be lauded, or not blamed; but when they cannot, and want to do it anyway, here is the error and the blame. If France therefore was able to attack Naples with its forces, it should have done so. If it was not able, it should not have divided it. And, if the division of Lombardy which he made with the Venetians merited excuse, because by means of it he put a foot in Italy, this merits blame, since it was not excused by that necessity.

Therefore, Louis had made these five errors: extinguished the lesser powers; increased in Italy the power of a powerful one; brought in a most powerful foreigner; did not come to live there; did not put colonies there. Which errors still, with him alive, might not have harmed him, had he not made the sixth: to take the state from the Venetians; because, had he not made the Church great nor put Spain into Italy, it would have been good and reasonable[58] and necessary to lower them; but having made these choices,[59]

56. "that." Between the commas Machiavelli writes only one word, *che*, meaning literally "so that." The implication is that Louis was so stupid as to compound a serious error with an even worse error.

57. In other words, fearing that Pope Alexander would take Tuscany, the king of France was forced to invade Italy. But he made another mistake. He shared Naples with the king of Spain, who became the natural recourse of anti-French sentiment and potentially fatal to French interests in Italy.

58. *ben ragionevole.*

59. *Decisions* translated from *partito* again.

he should never have consented to their[60] ruin; because, those[61] being powerful, they would always have kept others from trying to take Lombardy, whether because the Venetians would not have consented to such an enterprise without their becoming lords of it, whether because the others would not have wanted to take it from France to give it to them, and would not have had the spirit to go and bash against them both. And if someone were to say: King Louis yielded Romagna to Alexander and the kingdom[62] to Spain in order to avoid a war, I answer with the reasons said above: that one must never allow a disorder to continue in order to avoid a war; because it is not avoided but is deferred to your disadvantage. And if some others were to bring up the faith[63] that the king had given to the pope, to do that enterprise for him in exchange for the dissolution of his marriage and the hat[64] of Rouen; I answer with that which will be said by me below about the faith of princes and how one should observe it. King Louis thus lost Lombardy because he failed to observe any of the terms observed by others who took provinces and wanted to keep them. Nor is this any miracle, but very ordinary and reasonable. And I spoke of this matter with Rouen at Nantes, when Valentino — for thus Cesare Borgia, son of Pope Alexander, was commonly known — was occupying Romagna: because the cardinal of Rouen was telling me that the Italians were not competent in war, I answered him that the French are not competent in state; because if they were, they would not leave the Church in such greatness. And through experience it has been seen that the greatness in Italy, both of the latter and of Spain, has been caused by France, and its ruin[65] caused by them. From which one draws a general rule, which never or rarely fails: that whoever is the cause of one becoming powerful, is ruined; because that power is caused by him either by industriousness or by force, and both of these are suspect to whomever has become powerful.

60. The Venetians'.

61. The Venetians.

62. of Naples.

63. I.e., the pledge. Note Machiavelli's forced use of the word *faith* to describe an ordinary political deal involving the Church.

64. A cardinal's hat.

65. Italy's ruin.

IV

Cur Darii regnum quod Alexander occupaverat a successoribus suis post Alexandri mortum non defecit

(Why the kingdom of Darius, which was occupied by Alexander, did not defect from his successors after Alexander's death)

Considering the difficulty one has in keeping a newly acquired state, one could marvel whence it sprang that Alexander the Great became lord of Asia in a few years and, having only just occupied it, died; whence it seemed reasonable that all that state might rebel; nonetheless, Alexander's successors kept it for themselves, and had no other difficulties in keeping it than that which sprang up among themselves because of their own ambition. I answer that the principalities of which one has memory are governed in two different ways: either by a prince while all the other are servants, and by those who, as ministers, help to govern that kingdom by his grace and concession; or by one prince and by barons, who hold that rank not by the grace of the lord but because of the antiquity of their bloodlines. Such barons have their own states and subjects, who recognize them as lords and have natural affection for them. Those states which are governed by one prince and by servants, have a prince with greater authority; because in all the province no one but him is recognized as superior and, if they obey any other, they do it as minister and official,[66] and do not bear him particular love.

The examples of these two kinds of governments in our time are the Turk and the king of France. All the monarchy of the Turk is governed by one lord: the others are his servants: and, distinguishing his kingdom into

66. That is, they obey him because of the office to which the prince has appointed him, not because of who he is.

Sanjaks,[67] he sends different administrators there, and shifts and changes them as it pleases him. But the king of France is placed in the middle of an ancient multitude of lords recognized in that state by their subjects and loved by them: they have their preeminences: the king cannot take them away without danger to himself. Therefore, whoever considers both these states will find difficulty in acquiring the state of the Turk but, be it won, great ease in keeping it.[68] The causes of the difficulties involved in occupying the kingdom of the Turk are the impossibility of being called into it by the princes of that kingdom. Nor can one hope to facilitate the enterprise through the rebellion of those he has around him: which springs from the aforesaid reasons. Because they are all enslaved and obligated to him, they can be corrupted with greater difficulty; and, even when they be corrupted, one can hope little of them that is useful, since they are unable to carry the peoples with them for the reasons indicated. Therefore, whoever attacks the Turk must think of finding him united; and he had better[69] hope more in his own forces than in the disorders of others. But if he be vanquished and broken in the field so that he is not able to remake armies, one has to fear nothing but the bloodline of the prince: which, once extinguished, no one is left to fear, the others not having credit[70] with the peoples: and, as the winner could not hope in them[71] before victory, so after it he does not have to fear them.

The contrary occurs in kingdoms governed like that of France, because you can enter there with ease, gaining for yourself some baron of the kingdom; because always one finds malcontents and some who want to innovate. These, for the said reasons, can open for you the way to that state and facilitate your victory; which thereafter, wanting to maintain yourself,

67. "distinguendo el suo regno in Sangiachi." The Sanjaks were the appointed governors of Turkish provinces, which also bore the name. Machiavelli does not say that the Turk *divided* his kingdom among his governors. The lines drawn on the map of a unitary state represent nothing more than the will of the sovereign. They are not *divisions* which in any way exist outside the sovereign's will. Therefore, when a sovereign so parcels his domain, he does not actually divide but merely *distinguishes*. Likwise, in our time the decentralization of centralized states must be understood very differently from the local liberties of true federal systems.

68. Some versions of the text continue: "thus on the contrary you will find for some reasons greater ease in occupying the state of France, but great difficulty in keeping it."

69. The expression is *Li conviene*, "it is convenient to him."

70. *Credito*, i.e., "credibility" or "standing."

71. The people.

entails infinite difficulties, both with those who have helped you and with those whom you have oppressed. Nor is it enough for you to extinguish the bloodline of the prince, because there remain those lords who make themselves heads of new efforts at change; and, not being able either to make them content or to extinguish them, you lose the state whenever the occasion comes.

Now, if you[72] will consider what kind of government was that of Darius, you[73] will find it similar to the kingdom of the Turk; and therefore it was necessary for Alexander first to strike it all and take the field from it; after which victory, Darius being dead, that state remained secure for Alexander for the above mentioned reasons. And his successors, had they been united, could have enjoyed it lazily: nor did other tumults spring up in that kingdom than those which they themselves raised up. But it is impossible to possess with such quiet states ordered like that of France. From this sprang the frequent rebellions of Spain, of France, and of Greece against the Romans, because of the thick[74] principalities that were in those states; while the memory of which lasted, the Romans were always uncertain of their possession; but when the memory of them was extinguished by the power and long duration of the empire, they became their secure possessors. And thereafter, fighting among themselves, they[75] also were able each to carry with him part of those provinces, according to the authority he had taken therein; and since the bloodline of their ancient lord had been extinguished, these[76] recognized none but the Romans. Considering these things, therefore, no one will marvel at the ease which Alexander had in keeping the state of Asia, and of the difficulties that he and others have had in keeping what is acquired,[77] like Phyrrus and many [others]. This springs not from the great or small virtue of the winner, but from the disparity of the subject matter.

72. Formal or plural "you."

73. Again, the formal usage.

74. *Spessi*, thick, in the sense that grass is thick. Earlier in this sentence, the adjective modifying rebellions is *spesse*, translated as "frequent."

75. The Romans.

76. Provinces.

77. Acquired, that is, in Europe.

V

Quomodo administrandae sint civitates vel principatus, qui antequam occuparentur suis legibus vivebant

(In what way are to be administered the cities or principalities which, before being occupied, lived by their own laws)

When the states which one acquires, as is said, are used to living with their laws and in liberty, there are three ways to keep them: the first, to ruin them; the other, to go to live there personally; the third, to let them live with their laws, taking from them an annuity and creating therein a state of the few which might keep it friendly to you. Because, that state being created by that prince, it knows that it cannot be without his friendship and power and must do everything to maintain him. And one more easily keeps a city used to living free through its citizens, assuming one wants to preserve it.

In exemplis[78] there are the Spartans and the Romans. The Spartans kept Athens and Thebes, creating a state of the few there; nonetheless, they lost them again. The Romans, to keep Capua, Carthage, and Numantia, undid them[79] and did not lose them. They wanted to keep Greece much in the way the Spartans had held it,[80] making it free and leaving its laws; and it did not succeed for them; so that they were constrained to undo many cities of that province in order to keep it. Because, in truth, there is no secure way to possess them other than ruin. And whoever becomes lord of a city ac-

---

78. Latin, "for example."

79. The Romans drew the plow over Carthage in 146 B.C. and over Numantia in 133. Capua, however, was wholly destroyed only in a sociopolitical sense in 211 B.C.

80. Sparta imposed the government of the "Thirty Tyrants" on Athens at the end of the Peloponnesian War in 404 B.C. Thrasybulus overthrew this regime in 403. Thebes had a like regime imposed on it in 382 B.C. and overthrew it in 379.

customed to living free and does not undo her, he may expect to be undone by her; because in rebellion it always has for a refuge the name of liberty and of its ancient orders; which one never forgets either because of the passage of time or because of [the ruler's] beneficence. And whatever one might do or provide, if one does not disunite or disperse the inhabitants, they do not forget that name nor those orders, and suddenly in every accident they come back; as did Pisa after a hundred years that she had been put in serfdom by the Florentines.[81] But when cities or provinces are used to living under a prince, and [when] that bloodline is extinguished, on the one hand being used to obeying, on the other not having the old prince, they do not agree to make [a prince] from among themselves; also, since they do not know how to live free, they are slower to take arms, and a prince can gain them and make sure of them with greater ease. But in the republics there is greater life, greater hate, more desire of vengeance; neither does it leave, nor can it let rest the memory of ancient liberty: so it is that the most certain path is to extinguish them or to live there.

81. Acquired in 1405, rebelled in 1494.

VI

De principatibus novis qui armis propriis et virtute acquiruntur
(Of the new principalities which are acquired with one's own arms and virtue)

Let no one marvel if, in speaking of principalities wholly new in both prince and state,[82] I will point to very great examples; because since men almost always walk the paths beaten by others and go about their actions by imitation, unable either wholly to keep the ways of others or to add to the virtue of those whom you imitate, a prudent man must always enter by the paths beaten by great men and imitate those who have been most excellent, so that, if his own virtue does not reach it,[83] at least it might be able to yield some of its scent: and do like prudent archers who, the place where they intend[84] to wound seeming too far, and knowing how far the virtue of their bow reaches, aim much higher than the destined place, not to reach such height with their arrow, but in order to be able to attain their design[85] with the aid of such high aim. I say, therefore, that in wholly new principalities, where there is a new prince, there is more or less difficulty in maintaining them, according to whether he who acquires them is more or less virtuous. And because this event, becoming a prince from a private individual, presupposes either virtue or fortune, it seems that either of these things might partly mitigate many difficulties: nonetheless, whoever has stood[86] less on fortune has maintained himself more. It also makes for ease if the prince, not having other states, is constrained to come to live there

82. New with respect to dynasty and political organization.

83. The virtue of the great.

84. *Disegnano*, "design" or "scheme," third person plural.

85. *Disegno*, "design," here means "scheme." Note that Machiavelli does not use any of the many Italian words that connote narrow objectives, such as "target." His archer is aiming at comprehensive schemes.

86. Literally, "was" (*è stato*), meaning "has relied."

personaliter.[87] But to come to those who became princes by their own virtue and not because of them,[88] I say that the most excellent ones are Moses, Cyrus, Romulus, Theseus, and the like. And although one may not reason[89] of Moses, he having been a mere executor of the things which were ordered him by God, *tamen*[90] he must be admired *solum*[91] for that grace which made him worthy of speaking with God. But let us consider Cyrus and the others who acquired or founded kingdoms: you[92] will find them all admirable; and if their particular actions and orders are considered, they will appear not different from those of Moses, who had such a great preceptor.[93] *Et*[94] examining their actions and life, one does not see that they had other from fortune than the occasion, which gave them the matter into which they could introduce what form they liked; and without that occasion the virtue of their spirit would have extinguished itself, and without that virtue the occasion would have come in vain. It was therefore necessary for Moses to find the people of Israel, in Egypt, slaves and oppressed by the Egyptians, so that the former, in order to come out of servitude, might dispose themselves to follow him. For Romulus to become king of Rome and founder of that fatherland, it was necessary[95] that Romulus not be confined[96] in Alba, that he should have been exposed at birth.[97] It was

87. Latin, "personally." Notice the string of Latin terms that begins here. Machiavelli is highlighting a point with mock solemnity.

88. *Quelle*, "them," refers to "virtue" or "fortune." Note well: Machiavelli is counterposing "virtue" to the virtue by which private men become princes. Other texts have "fortune" instead of "them." This is a clear contraposition between one's own virtue and fortune.

89. The prohibition is stated in the subjunctive, *"non si debba ragionare."*

90. Latin, "nevertheless" or "despite the foregoing."

91. Latin, "alone" or "only." The mock solemnity is unmistakable.

92. Plural.

93. Namely, God.

94. Latin, "and." After God, more mock solemnity.

95. *Conveniva.* Here the verb *convenire* is used in the sense of necessary relationship. Machiavelli makes a wickedly humorous contrast with the other meaning of the word expressed by the third object of the sentence (fn. 97): It was "convenient" that Romulus be exposed at birth.

96. *Non capissi* (subjunctive), i.e., not be in a place capable of holding his greatness.

97. According to legend, a jealous king of Alba ordered the twins Romulus and Remus to be put out to die. A she-wolf found the babies in a swamp next to the Tiber, suckled them, and raised them. That spot, now in downtown Rome, has been known since

necessary that Cyrus should find the Persians discontented in the empire of the Medes, and the Medes soft and effeminate because of a long peace. Theseus could not demonstrate his virtue if he did not find the Athenians dispersed. These occasions consequently made these men happy, and their excellent virtue enabled them to recognize that occasion whence the fatherland was ennobled and became most happy.

Those who, by virtuous ways similar to these, become princes acquire the principality with difficulty but keep it with ease; and the difficulties they have in acquiring the principality spring in part from the new orders and modes that they are forced to introduce in order to found their state and their security. And it must be considered that nothing is more difficult to transact, nor more dubious to succeed, nor more dangerous to manage, than to make oneself chief to introduce new orders. Because the introducer has for enemies all those whom the old orders benefit, and has for lukewarm defenders all those who might benefit by the new orders. Which lukewarmness springs in part from the fear of adversaries who have the laws on their side, in part from the incredulity of men, who do not truly believe in new things if they do not see solid experience born of them. From which it follows that whenever those who are enemies have the occasion to attack, they do it in a partisan manner, while those others defend tepidly; so that alongside them one is imperiled. It is necessary to discuss this part well, however, to examine whether such innovators stand by themselves or depend on others; that is, if in order to accomplish such work they need to pray[98] or can truly force. In the first case they always end up badly and do not accomplish anything; but when they depend on their own [strength], then they are rarely imperiled. From this it comes that all armed prophets won and the unarmed came to ruin. Because, beyond the things said, the nature of peoples is variable; and it is easy to persuade them of something, but it is difficult to fix them in that persuasion. And therefore it is necessary[99] to be prepared so that, when they no longer believe, one might make them believe by force. Moses, Cyrus, Theseus, and Romulus would not have been able to make them observe their constitutions for long had they been unarmed; as in our

---

the eighth century B.C. as the Lupercalia. Note Machiavelli's superciliousness: misfortunes, including being put out to die at birth, are supposed to be necessary occasions for the development of virtue. The point of Chap. VI, however, is to define the virtue of founders. This has everything to do with inflicting adversity, not suffering it.

98. *Preghino* means both to plead with or to convince men, and to pray to God. Machiavelli clearly intends the double meaning. The reader can see him chuckle as he wrote.

99. *Conviene.*

times happened[100] to Friar Girolamo Savonarola; who came to ruin in his new orders, as the multitude began not to believe them; and he did not have a way to hold firm those who had believed, nor to make the unbelievers believe. Because of this, such [unarmed prophets] have great difficulty in proceeding, and all dangers are in their way, and it is necessary[101] that they overcome them with virtue; but, having overcome them and, when they begin to be venerated, having extinguished those who envied their station,[102] they remain powerful, secure, honored, and happy.

To such high examples I want to add a minor example; but well[103] it has some proportion with the former; and I want that it suffice me for all other similar ones; and this is Hiero of Syracuse.[104] This private man became prince of Syracuse: neither did he get any more from fortune than the occasion; because, the Syracusans being oppressed, they elected him their captain; from which he merited to be made their prince. And he was of such virtue, *etiam*[105] while a private citizen, that he who writes of him says: "quod nihil illi deerat ad regnandum praeter regnum."[106] This man extinguished the old militia, ordered a new one; left old friendships, took up new ones; and, as he came to have friendships and soldiers that were his own, was able to build every edifice on that foundation; all of which took him much effort to acquire and little to maintain.

100. Literally, "intervened." Girolamo Savanarola (1452–1498), a Dominican priest who preached fiery sermons against the worldliness of Church and nobles, and who founded the Florentine Republic (1494–1498), was burned at the stake after the people grew tired of him and blamed him for their defeats.

101. *Conviene.*

102. Literally, "quality." Power, security, honor, happiness come once they have snuffed out those who envied their "quality," meaning their virtue or their qualitative status. Machiavelli is ambiguous.

103. *Bene*, also good.

104. Note the assertive tone. Hiero II (306–215 B.C.), one of Pyrrhus's lieutenants, became chief of the Syracusan army and took over the city in 265. He is a textbook example of a tyrant. Earlier, Machiavelli had solemnly said that "the most excellent" founders were Moses, Cyrus, et al. and that the others' ways were "not different" from Moses's, who was God's executor. But he said nothing about Moses's nor anybody else's virtue. Now he talks about the founders' virtue and gives us only one example, which he wants to stand for "all other similar ones" — Hiero's virtue is no different from Moses's or God's.

105. Latin, "as well."

106. Latin, "It seemed that he lacked nothing to reign except a kingdom." Again, solemnity. But the following sentence encapsulates Machiavelli's understanding of political virtue.

VII

De principatibus novis qui alienis armis et fortuna acquiruntur
(Of new principalities that are acquired by means of the arms of others and by fortune)

Those private men who become princes by fortune alone do it with little effort but maintain themselves with much; and they have no difficulty on the way, because they fly there: but all the difficulties spring up when they are in place. And such are when a state is conceded to someone either for money or by the grace of him who concedes it: as happened to many in Greece, in the cities of Ionia and of the Hellespont, where they were made princes by Darius so that they might hold them for his safety and glory; as also those were made emperors who came to the emperorship from private station through the corruption of the soldiers. Such princes stand[107] simply upon the will and fortune of whoever conceded it to them, which are two most voluble and unstable things: and they do not know how and they have not the power to hold that rank: they do not know, because, if he is not a man of great genius and virtue, it is not reasonable that, having always lived in private fortune, he knows how to command; they cannot, because they do not have forces that might be friendly and faithful to them. Moreover, the states that come right away, like all other things of nature that are born and grow fast, cannot have their roots and connections,[108] so that the first ad-

107. The verb is *stare*, which means "to be" in particular, variable circumstances, like the Spanish verb *estar*. The image is of princes who stand on precarious footing.

108. The word *barbe* literally means "beards." Farmers use it to refer to fine roots. Nevertheless, young men who lack experience are also said not to have yet grown a beard. The word thus might well be understood to mean human experience, and the word *correspondenzie*, connections, understood in a human sense. Lisio, on the other hand, is quite clear in his opinion that both *barbe* and *correspondenzie* refer to vegetable matter. The question cannot be decided by the meaning of the word *tempo*, which means "time" as well as "weather." There would be, therefore, no more evidence to support the conten-

verse circumstances[109] extinguish them; if yet those who, as is said, have become princes so rapidly are not equal to that which fortune placed in their lap, let them know right away to prepare themselves to preserve it and let them afterward make those foundations that the others had made before they became princes.

To both of these aforementioned ways, about becoming a prince by virtue or fortune, I want to attach two examples which have been[110] in the days of our memory: and these are Francesco Sforza and Cesare Borgia. Francesco, by the appropriate means[111] and with great virtue, became duke of Milan from private station, and he kept with little effort that which he had acquired with a thousand gasps.[112] On the other hand, Cesare Borgia, called Duke Valentino by the people, acquired the state with the fortune of the father, and with that he lost it; even though for him every device was used[113] and all those things were done[114] which should have been done by a prudent and virtuous man to sink his roots[115] into states that the arms and the fortune of others had conceded to him. Because, as was said above, whoever does not make the foundations first might make them later with great virtue, though doing so then entails discomfort to the architect and danger to the edifice. If then one will consider all the duke's proceedings, one will see how he made for himself great foundation for future power: which I do not

---

tion that Machiavelli was thinking of human affairs than of vegetable matter except for the final word in the phrase, "extinguish," a common euphemism for killing, which simply is inapplicable to uprooted plants.

109. *Tempo* means either time (i.e., human circumstance) or weather.

110. In this awkward, contrived expression, *esempli stati* can mean, literally, exemplary states. Hence, the sentence means not just that these two examples have existed in recent times, but that the tyrants Sforza and Borgia were exemplary. Later in the paragraph it becomes clear that Borgia is the paragon of Machiavellian virtue.

111. *Debiti* means literally "debts." The means would then be the ones owed to the situation. The word is also related to *dovuti*, which gives the same meaning, i.e., "appropriate." The means themselves were a combination of deceit and voilence, as Machiavelli tells us in *The Prince*, Chap. XIV, *The History of Florence*, Bk. VI, and *The Art of War*, Bk. I.

112. I.e., with a lot of hard breathing.

113. *Si usassi*, impersonal form, subjunctive mood. It is therefore not clear whether the foregoing *per* means "for" or "by."

114. Subjunctive once again, "all those things" are done *per* a prudent and virtuous man.

115. *barbe*, here meaning unequivocally "roots."

judge it superfluous to discuss, because I would not know better precepts to give to a new prince than the example of his actions: and if his orders[116] did not profit him, it was not his fault, because it originated from an extraordinary and extreme malignity of fortune.

Many difficulties present and future stood in the way of Alexander the Sixth's desire to make great his son the duke. First, he did not see a way to make him lord of any state that was not a state of the Church, and he knew that the duke of Milan and the Venetians would not allow him to take from that[117] of the Church because Faenza and Rimini were already under the protection of the Venetians. Beyond this he saw that the armies of Italy, and especially those of which he could have made use, were in the hands of those who had to fear the greatness of the pope; and therefore he could not trust them, being all with the Orsini and Colonnesi[118] and their accomplices. It was therefore necessary that those orders be disturbed, and [it was necessary] to disorder their[119] states, in order to be able securely to take power for oneself over part of them. Which turned out to be easy for him because he found the Venetians who, moved by other causes, had turned to making the French pass into Italy again: which he[120] not only did not interdict but rather facilitated with the dissolution of King Louis' old marriage. The king therefore passed into Italy with the help of the Venetians and the consent of Alexander; nor was he in Milan before the pope had people[121] from him for the enterprise in Romagna; which[122] was consented to him because of the reputation of the king. Therefore, the duke, having acquired Romagna and beaten the Colonnesi, wanted to keep the former and to proceed further. Two things impeded him: one was his armies, which did not seem trustworthy to him, and the other the will of France; that is, that the Orsini armies, whose worth he had gauged, might go out from under him and not only might impede his acquiring but might take from him what had been acquired, and that the king might yet do the same. Of the Orsini he had a token when, after the taking of Faenza, he attacked Bo-

116. I.e., the means he employed.

117. That state, including Faenza and Rimini.

118. Two noble families that contended for power in the city of Rome and over the papal states.

119. The states belonging to the Orsini and Colonnesi families.

120. Pope Alexander.

121. I.e., armies.

122. Romagna. That is, because people realized that the king of France was backing the pope, Romagna's resistance to the pope collapsed.

logna, because he saw them go cold in that attack; and about the king he came to know his spirit[123] when, having taken the duchy of Urbino, he attacked Tuscany: from which enterprise he was made to desist by the king. Because of this the duke decided not to depend any more on the arms and fortunes of others. And, first thing, he weakened the Orsini and Colonnesi parties in Rome; because he earned to himself all their adherents, clansmen[124] though they might have been, making them his clansmen and giving them stipends; and he honored them, according to their qualities, with captaincies and government posts: so that in a few months the affection of the parties extinguished itself and wholly turned upon the duke. After this, he waited for the occasion to extinguish the Orsini, having dispersed those of the Colonna house; which[125] came well to him, and he used it better; because the Orsini, having recognized late that the greatness of the duke and of the Church was their ruin, made a conclave at the Magione,[126] in the Perugia region. From the latter sprang the rebellion of Urbino and the tumults of Romagna and infinite dangers to the duke, all of which he overcame with the help of the French. And, his reputation having returned to him, neither trusting France nor other external sources, he turned to ruses in order not to be compelled to a showdown with them. And he knew so well how to dissimulate his spirit that the Orsini reconciled themselves to him through Lord Paulo, whom the duke did not fail in every kind of act to reassure, giving him monies, clothes, and horses; so that their simplicity led them to Sinigallia into his hands.[127] Then, having extinguished these chiefs and having reduced their partisans to being his friends, having all of Romagna with the duchy of Urbino, the duke had laid good enough foundations for his power, it seeming to him that he had acquired Romagna as a friend and had earned for himself all those peoples, enough to have begun to taste their well-being.[128]

And because this part is worth being known and imitated by others, I do

123. Machiavelli means "intention." But he uses the word *animo* (spirit), which is close to *anima* (soul), in bitter mockery of a churchman who claimed to be searching the souls of men.

124. *Gentili* (adjective) means of the same *gens*, that is, men having blood ties.

125. Occasion.

126. A village near Perugia, on 9 October 1502.

127. Vitellozzo Vitelli and Oliverotto de Fermo, along with many others, were killed at the meeting in Sinigallia on 31 December 1502, when Borgia's soldiers cut them down after dinner. In January 1503, Paolo Orsini fell into a similar trap at Castel della Pieve.

128. I.e., tasting the material benefits and the power of his conquests.

not want to leave it behind. Having taken Romagna and finding it commanded by impotent lords who would sooner despoil their subjects than govern them, and [who had] given them occasion for disunity, not for unity, so that the whole province was full of thefts, feuds, and every other kind of insolence, he judged it necessary, in order to render it peaceful and obedient to the sovereign arm, to give it good government. Therefore, he put at its head[129] Remirro de Orco, cruel and expeditious man; to him he gave the fullest power. This one in little time rendered it peaceful and united, with the greatest reputation. Thereafter the duke judged such excessive authority not to be necessary, because he feared it might become hateful; and he proposed there[130] a civil judiciary[131] in the middle of the province, with a most excellent president, where each city had its own advocate. And because he knew the past rigors had generated some hate, in order to purge the spirits of those peoples and to wholly gain them to himself, he wanted to show that if any cruelty had ensued, it had sprung not from him but from the brusque nature of the minister. And having taken this for his opportunity, he had him placed in the square in Cesena, one morning, in two pieces with a piece of wood and a bloody knife beside him. The ferocity of which spectacle left those peoples at once satisfied and stupefied.

But let us return whence we departed. I say that, the duke finding himself powerful enough and in part secured against present dangers, because he had armed himself in his way and had by and large extinguished those armies which, nearby, could have harmed him, there remained to him fear[132] of the king of France; because he wanted to proceed with acquisition and knew he would not be suffered by the king, who of late had become aware of his error. And because of this he began to seek new friendships, and to vacillate with France in the expedition which the French made to the Kingdom of Naples, against the Spanish who were besieging Gaeta. And his intention[133] was to make sure of them: which soon would have succeeded for him if Alexander had lived.

And these were his dispositions regarding present things. But as far as

129. *Vi prepose*, "he pre-posed there," i.e., he put forth or placed at the head of the government.

130. *Propose vi*, "proposed there," a neat linguistic reversal on his installation of de Orco. Having imposed brutally, Borgia could now be sure that his evil magistrates would be accepted and obeyed.

131. I.e., an assembly of the leading citizenry.

132. *Rispetto*, respect.

133. *Animo*, "spirit," here means that his mind was quickened by the intention.

the future ones, he had in the first instance to ponder lest a new successor to the Church not be his friend and try to take from him what Alexander had given him; and he thought to do it[134] in four ways: first, to take that opportunity from the pope, by extinguishing all the bloodlines of those lords whom he had despoiled; second, to earn for himself all the gentile men of Rome, as is said,[135] in order to be able to keep the pope in check with them; third, to make the College of Cardinals as much his as he could; fourth, to acquire so much power before the pope died that he might resist a first attack by himself alone. Of these four things, at the death of Alexander, he had made three happen, the fourth he considered almost done: because of the despoiled lords he killed as many as he could reach, and very few saved themselves; the gentile Romans he had earned for himself, and he had a very great party in the college;[136] and as for a new acquisition, he had schemed to become lord of Tuscany, and already possessed Perugia and Piombino, and had taken up Pisa's protectorate. And because he did not have to have respect for France (which he did not have to have any longer, since the French had already been despoiled of the kingdom[137] by the Spaniard, so that each of them was constrained by necessity to buy his friendship), he was jumping on Pisa. After this, Lucca and Siena gave up right away, in part out of envy of the Florentines, in part out of fear; the Florentines had no remedy; [so that] if he had succeeded (which would have happened the same year Alexander died), he would have acquired for himself so many forces and so much reputation that he could have held himself up and would no longer have depended on the forces and fortunes of others, but on his own power and virtue. But Alexander died five years after he had begun to draw the sword. He left him with only the state of Romagna solidified, with all the others up in the air, in between two most powerful armies, and sick to death. And there was so much ferocity and so much virtue in the duke, and so well did he know how men are to be gained or to be lost, and so valid were the foundations which in so little time he had made for himself, that, if he had not had those armies on him, or if he had

134. That is, the result of his pondering was a decision to secure himself against the new pope's possible unfriendliness by doing four things.

135. The "as is said" tends to confirm that he is using the word *gentili* in its primordial connotation of "clan." See Chap. VII above. It also refers to the combination of fraud and murder by which Borgia had mastered the Orsini and Colonnesi.

136. The College of Cardinals, which elects a new pope after the previous pope's death.

137. The Kingdom of Naples.

been well, he would have withstood every difficulty. And one saw that his foundations were good; because Romagna waited for him more than a month; in Rome, though half-alive, he remained secure, and even though Ballioni, Vitelli, and Orsini came to Rome, they had no following against him; he was able, if not to make pope whomever he wanted, at least to block whomever he did not want. Had he been healthy at Alexander's death, everything would have been easy for him. And he told me in the days in which Julius II was created[138] that he had thought about[139] what might happen as a result of his father's death, and he found a remedy for everything, except that he never thought of his[140] death, that he himself also was about to die.

Therefore I, having drawn together all the duke's actions, would not know to gainsay him; on the contrary, it seems [proper] to me to set him forth[141] as I have done as imitable by all who have risen to power by fortune or by the arms of others. Because he, having great spirit and high intentions, could not have behaved otherwise; and only the brevity of Alexander's life and his illness opposed themselves to his schemes. Whoever therefore judges it necessary in his new principality to secure himself against enemies, to earn friends, to vanquish by force or fraud, to make himself loved and feared by peoples, to be followed and revered by soldiers, to extinguish those who can or must harm you,[142] to innovate the ancient orders with new modes, to be severe and gracious, magnanimous and liberal, to extinguish the unfaithful militia, create a new one, keep friendships of kings and princes, so that they might have either to benefit you with grace or to harm you with respect, cannot find fresher examples than his actions. One can only accuse him in the creation of Julius as pontiff, in which he elected badly; because, as is said, not being able to make the pope he wanted, he could always obtain[143] that anyone not be pope; and he never should have consented to the papacy of those cardinals whom he had harmed, or who,[144]

138. The word *creato*, created, in this context is as inappropriate and mocking in Italian as it is in English.

139. I.e., he had provided for.

140. "His" may refer to his father's death or to his own. It is grammatically — and, therefore, otherwise — ambiguous.

141. *Preporlo*, rare, and easily interchangeable with the common *proporlo*, "propose him." Machiavelli used the same word to indicate Cesare's installation of de Orco.

142. Familiar singular.

143. *Tenere* is probably a contraction of *ottenere*, "obtain."

144. "*O che, diventati papi, avessino ad avere.*" *Che* could be a contraction of

having become popes, would have to fear him. Because men do harm either for fear or for hate. Those whom he had harmed were, among others, San Pietro ad Vincula, Colonna, San Giorgio, Ascanio. All the others, having become popes, had to fear him, except Rouen and the Spaniards, the latter because of affinity and obligation, the former because of power, having joined himself to the kingdom of France. Therefore, before all things, the duke should have created a Spaniard pope, and, not being able to do that, should have consented that it be Rouen and not San Pietro ad Vincula. And whoever believes that in great personages new benefits might make old injuries forgotten, deceives himself. Therefore, the duke erred in his choice, and it was the cause of his final ruin.

---

perché, in which case the phrase should be translated "or because [he thought], having become popes, they might have to have." But this would conflict with the advice contained in the rest of the paragraph.

VIII

De his qui per scelera ad principatum pervenere (Of those who have come to princedom by iniquity)

But because one becomes a prince from private status in two other ways, which cannot wholly be attributed either to fortune or to virtue, it is unseemly to me[145] to leave them out, even though one of these may be more widely discussed where republics are treated.[146] These are when one rises to principality through some iniquitous and nefarious means, or when a private citizen becomes prince of his fatherland with the favor of fellow citizens. And, speaking of the first way, it will be shown with two examples, one ancient, the other modern, without otherwise entering into the merits of this part[147] why I judge it sufficient that whoever might be in need, imitate them.

Agathocles the Sicilian became king of Syracuse from a fortune [that was not only] private but lowly and abject. Born of a potter, this one always had an iniquitous life throughout his years: nonetheless, he accomplished his iniquities with such virtue of spirit and of body that, having joined the militia, he rose through its ranks to become *praetor*[148] of Syracuse. Being established in which rank, and having decided[149] to become prince and to keep with violence and without obligation to others what had been conceded him by agreement, and having an understanding concerning this design of his with Hamilcar the Carthaginian, who was operating with his

---

145. *non mi pare*, "it does not seem to me." This very common incomplete expression begs the question "why not?" The sense of the sentence, however, is that it is not seemly.

146. Namely, in Machiavelli's *Discourses*.

147. That is, Machiavelli claims to stay at arm's length from the question of whether this sort of thing is good. As we shall see, he is intimately involved.

148. Military commander.

149. *Deliberato*, "deliberated."

armies in Sicily, one morning he convened the people and the senate of Syracuse, as if he had had to deliberate[150] things pertinent to the republic; and at a preordained nod he had all the senators and the richest of the people killed by his soldiers. Once they were killed, he occupied and held the principality of that city without any civil controversy. And although he was twice routed[151] and finally besieged by the Carthaginians, he not only was able to defend his city but, having left part of his people to the defense of the siege, he attacked Africa with the others, and in a brief time freed Syracuse from the siege and militarily brought the Carthaginians to extreme necessity: and they were constrained to reconcile themselves with him, being content with the possession of Africa, and to leave Sicily to Agathocles. Therefore, whoever might consider this man's actions and virtues will see no things, or few, which he might attribute to fortune; thus, as is said above, he came to principality not through anyone's favor but through the ranks of the militia, which he had earned with a thousand discomforts and dangers, and thereafter he kept it with many animated and dangerous partisan struggles. One cannot yet call it virtue to kill one's own citizens, to betray friends, to be without faith, without pity, without religion, by which modes one can acquire empire, but not glory. Because, if one were to consider Agathocles' virtue in entering into and exiting from dangers, and the greatness of his spirit in bearing and overcoming adverse things, one does not see why he might have to be judged inferior to any most excellent captain. Nonetheless, his ferocious cruelty and inhumanity, with infinite iniquities, do not consent that he be celebrated among the most excellent men. One cannot therefore attribute to fortune or virtue what he achieved without one or the other.

In our times, Alexander VI reigning, Oliverotto da Fermo, having been orphaned[152] many years before, was raised by a maternal uncle named Giovanni Fogliani, and in his earliest youth given to military service under Paolo Vitelli, so that, filled with that discipline, he might attain to some excellent military rank. Thereafter, Paolo dead, he served under his brother,

150. *Deliberare*. But he had already deliberately planned a slaughter. Note the ironic double meaning.

151. That is, defeated in battle.

152. The word Machiavelli uses here for orphan is *piccolo*, "small." This is a rare usage of the word indeed, but it points to Oliverotto's small stature and to what finally was his insufficiency. Agothocles was "big" with regard to the things in which Oliverotto was "small."

Vitellozzo, and in the briefest time, being astute and bold in person and in spirit, he became the first man in his militia. But, it seeming to him a servile thing to stay with others, he thought,[153] with the help of some citizens of Fermo, to whom serfdom was dearer than the liberty of their fatherland, and with Vitellozzo's indulgence, to occupy Fermo. And he wrote to Giovanni Fogliani how, having been away from home for many years, he wanted to come see him and his city, and in some way to come to know his patrimony again: and because he had labored for nothing else than to gain honor, he wanted to come in honor and accompanied by a hundred horsemen of his friends and servants, so that his citizens might see how he had not spent time in vain: and he begged that Giovanni might be pleased to order that he might be received honorably by the Fermians: which would honor not only himself but also Giovanni, he being his pupil. Therefore, Giovanni did not fail any act due to the nephew; and, having had him received honorfully by the Fermians, he[154] lodged himself in his houses: where, having passed some days and waited to order what was necessary to his future iniquity, he made a most solemn banquet, where he invited Giovanni Fogliani and all the first men of Fermo. And once the foods were consumed and all the other entertainments which are customary in similar banquets, Oliverotto artfully moved certain grave arguments, speaking of the greatness of Pope Alexander and of his son Cesare, and of their enterprises. Giovanni and the others answering which arguments, he at once rose up, saying that these things [were] to be spoken of in a more secret place; and he retired to a chamber, whereinto Giovanni and all the other citizens followed. Neither had they seated themselves before soldiers came out from its secret places who killed Giovanni and all the others. After which homicide, Oliverotto mounted horse and ran the land, and besieged the supreme magistrate in the palace; so much that out of fear they were constrained to obey him and to establish[155] a government, of which he made himself the prince. And all those being dead who could have harmed him, because they were unhappy with him, he fortified[156] himself with the new civil and military orders; so that, in the space of the year in which he held the principality, he not only

153. Note the parallel usage of *deliberare*. Oliverotto tried to think like Agathocles, but he was not in the same league. Cesare Borgia, however, was.

154. Now referring to Oliverotto, not to the uncle.

155. The word is *fermare*, which literally means "to stop." This unusual usage is a pun on the name of the city, Fermo.

156. *si corroboró*, i.e., fortified himself.

was secure in the city of Fermo but had become fearsome to all his neighbors. And his expunging would have been difficult, as was Agathocles', had he not let himself be duped by Cesare Borgia, when, as was said above, he took the Orsini and Vitelli in Sinigallia; where, one year after he had committed the parricide, he, together with Vitellozzo, who had been his teacher in his virtues and iniquities, was taken and strangled.

Someone could doubt whence it might spring that Agathocles and some similar was able to live long and secure in his fatherland after infinite betrayals and cruelty, and to defend himself from external enemies, and was never conspired against by his citizens: while[157] many others have not been able to maintain the state[158] through cruelty even in peaceful times, not to speak of the doubtful times of war. I believe that this might ensue from cruelties badly used or well used.[159] Well used one can call those[160] (if it is licit to say *bene*[161] of evil) which one does in one stroke, out of the necessity of assuring oneself, and thereafter are not persisted in, but are converted into as great usefulness as possible for the subjects. Badly used are those which, though yet in the beginning they be few, rather increase with time than flicker out. Those who observe the first mode can have some remedy for their state with God and with men; as Agathocles had.[162] Those others, it is impossible that they maintain themselves. Hence it is to be noted that, in taking a state, its occupier must consider all those offenses which it is necessary for him to do, and do them all in one stroke, in order not to have to renew them every day, and not renewing them to reassure men and to earn them to himself by benefiting them. Whoever does otherwise, either out of timidity or because of bad counsel, is always constrained to keep the knife in hand; nor can he ever base himself upon his subjects, these not being able to be sure of him because of the fresh and continuous injuries. Because injuries must be done all together, so that, being tasted less, they offend less: and the benefits must be done little by little so that they might be better

157. *Con cio sia che*, "with thus it be that," i.e., while.

158. *Stato* can mean polity, sociopolitical status, personal, or even marital status.

159. Here Machiavelli uses *bene* and *male*, good and evil, as adverbs to mean "well" and "badly." This is the point where Machiavelli begins the transformation of their meaning — a transformation that is at the very heart of his purpose in *The Prince*.

160. Treasons and cruelties.

161. Good.

162. No one but Machiavelli in this sentence even suggested that Agathocles ever endeared himself to God in any way.

tasted. And a prince must above all live with his subjects so that no accident either, ill or good, might constrain him to change: because, when necessities come through adverse times, you will not be in time with evil,[163] and the good you do does not benefit you, because it is judged to have been forced, and no gratitude at all is reserved you.[164]

163. I.e., you will not have time to maintain yourself by doing harm.

164. Most Italian authorities understand the last phrase as I have translated it. However, there is a minority position of which the reader should be aware. The last phrase contains two words, the meanings of which are uncertain, *grado* and *saputo*. The first is generally believed to be miswritten *grato*, or "gratitude." But if it is not miswritten, it means "rank." *Saputo* is likewise held to be used to mean *serbato*, "reserved." But if the word means "known," as it literally does, then the last phrase would have to mean "and no rank at all is recognized you." In either case the thrust of the sentence is the same.

IX

De principatu civili
(Of the civil principality)

But, coming to the other part, when a private citizen becomes prince of his fatherland not by iniquity or other intolerable violence but by the favor of other citizens, which one can call civil principality (neither all virtue nor all fortune is necessary to achieve it, but rather a fortunate cleverness), I say that one ascends to this principality either with the favor of the people or with the favor of the great. Because in every city one finds these two different dispositions,[165] and it springs from this that the people desire not to be commanded nor oppressed by the great, and that the great desire to command and oppress the people: and from these two different appetites one of three effects springs up in the city: either principality or liberty or license.

The principality is caused either by the people or by the great, according to whether one or the other of these parts has the occasion for it; because the great, seeing themselves[166] unable to resist the people, begin to devolve reputation to one among themselves and make him prince, so that they might vent their appetite under his shadow. The people, again, seeing themselves[167] unable to resist the great, devolve reputation to one and make him prince to be defended by his authority. He who comes to the principality with the help of the great maintains himself with greater difficulty than the one who becomes [prince] with the help of the people; because he finds himself prince with many around him who seem his equals, and because of this he can neither command them nor manage them his way. But he who arrives at the principality with popular favor finds himself there alone, and has around either no one or very few who are not ready to obey. Beyond this, one cannot satisfy the great honestly and without injury to others, but one can well [satisfy] the people; because the people's purpose is more honest than that of the great, the latter wanting to oppress and the former not to be oppressed. Furthermore, a prince can never secure himself against a hostile people, they being too many; against the great he can secure himself,

165. *Umori*, i.e., "humors" or "appetites."
166. The reflexive is the translator's.
167. Again, translator's reflexive.

they being few. The worst a prince might expect from a hostile people is to be abandoned by it; but from the great who are enemies, he must fear not only that he might be abandoned but also that they might come against him; because, there being more foresight and cunning in them, they always find occasion to rise up, and they seek rank from those they hope will win. Moreover, while it is always necessary for the prince to live with that same people, he can well do without those great ones, since he can make and unmake some of them every day, by taking away and giving them reputation at his pleasure.

And in order to better clear up this part, I say that one can consider the great principally in two ways. Either they conduct themselves so that by what they do they obligate themselves to your fortune completely, or not: those who do obligate themselves and are not rapacious, one must honor and love; those who do not obligate themselves must be examined in two ways. Either they do this out of pusillanimity and natural defect of the spirit. Then you must make use especially of those that are of good counsel, because in prosperous times they honor you and in adversities you do not have to fear them. But when they do not obligate themselves on purpose and because of ambition, it is a sign that they think more of themselves than of you; and the prince must guard himself against them, and fear them as if they were open enemies, because in adversities they will help ruin him.

Therefore, one who becomes prince through the favor of the people must keep it his friend: which should be easy, since it does not ask other than not to be oppressed. But one who becomes prince against the people with the favor of the great must try to earn the people to himself before anything else: which should be easy, if and when he takes up its protection. And because men, when they have good from him from whom they have expected evil, obligate themselves all the more to their benefactor, the people immediately become better disposed toward him than if he had made his way to the principality by its favors: and the prince can earn it in many ways, [concerning] which, because they vary according to the subject, one cannot give a sure rule, and therefore [they] will be left behind. I will conclude only that it is necessary for a prince to have the people as a friend: otherwise he has no remedy in adversity.

Nabis, prince of the Spartans, sustained the siege of all Greece and of a most victorious Roman army, and defended his fatherland and his state[168] against them, and when the danger came upon him, it sufficed him to secure himself against a few: which would not have sufficed him if he had had the

168. *Stato* here means Nabis's own political status.

people as enemy. And let no one reproach this opinion of mine with that
trite proverb, that he who builds upon the people builds upon mud: because
that is true when a private citizen makes his foundation on it, and lets
himself think[169] that the people might free him when he be oppressed by the
enemy or by the magistrates. In this case one could often find himself
deceived as were the Gracchi in Rome and Messer Georgio Scali in Firenze.
But if a prince were to found himself on it, as a prince able to command, and
as a man of heart, not dismayed in adversities, who did not lack other
preparations, and who moved the common people[170] with his spirit and
orders, never would he find himself deceived by it[171] and he would turn out
to have made his foundations well.

These principalities normally incur danger when they are about to rise
from civil into absolute order; because these princes command either by
themselves or by means of magistrates. In the last case their stance is
weaker and more dangerous; because they stand [or fall] wholly by the will
of those citizens who are set forth[172] in magistracies, who, especially in
adverse times, can take the state from him with great ease, either by going
against him or by not obeying him. And during dangers the prince lacks the
time to take up absolute authority; because the citizens and subjects, who
normally take orders from the magistrates, are not in these circumstances
disposed to obeying his; and in doubtful times he will always be destitute of
trustworthy people. Because such a prince cannot found himself upon what
he sees in quiet times, when the citizens have need of the state, because then
each runs, each promises, and each wants to die for him when death is far
away; but in adverse times, when the state has need of the citizens, then few
such people are to be found. And this experience is all the more dangerous
because it can be had but once. And therefore a wise prince must think of a
means by which his citizens have need of the state and of him, always and in
every kind of time, and then they will be faithful always.

169. Think wrongly, of course. The verb here is *dare da intendere*. Cf. note 6 above.

170. I.e., the whole people.

171. I.e., by the people.

172. *Preposti* — people to whom prominence has been given. The verb here is the
same as the one that described Cesare Borgia's appointment of Orco.

X

Quomodo omnium principatum vires perpendi debeant
(In what way the forces of all principalities must be measured)

In examining the qualities of these principalities, it is convenient[173] to have another consideration: that is, if a prince has so much state[174] that he may bear up by himself whenever he needs to, or rather if he always has need of defense by others. And to better clarify this part, I say that I judge able to bear themselves up by themselves those who can put together a proper army and make a day[175] with whomever comes to attack him because of abundance of either men or money, and hence I judge to always have need of others those who cannot show up against the enemy in the field, but are constrained to take refuge within the walls, and to guard them. I have discussed the first case, and in the future we will say of it what is necessary. Upon the second case, one cannot say more than to comfort[176] such princes to fortify and equip their own land[177] and to take no account of the countryside. And whoever will have fortified his own land well, and have handled himself as is said before and one will say below concerning the other measures, always will be attacked with great respect; because men are always against doing enterprises where difficulty may be seen, nor can one see ease in attacking one who has made his land valiant and is not hated by the people.

The cities of Germany are most free, have little countryside, and obey

173. *Conviene* (third per. sing.) implies that "one had better."

174. Here the ambiguity of *stato* is clear. It means both the provisions by which a man keeps his political primacy, and the means by which a polity maintains its political existence against others. *The Prince* talks about the nature of politics at all levels.

175. I.e., fight a set-piece battle.

176. The awkward expression *confortare* is deliberately weaker than "to advise" or "to urge." Princes who are in such straits are to be comforted to do something with little hope that doing it will save their necks.

177. I.e., city.

the emperor when they want to, and fear neither him nor any other powerful one they have around: because they are so fortified that each and every one thinks that expunging them would have to be tedious and difficult. Because all have moats and walls as they should,[178] and have enough artillery: they always keep in public storage enough to drink and to eat and to burn for one year; and beyond this, in order to be able to keep the plebs assuaged,[179] and without loss to the public, they always have in common enough to give them work for a year in those activities that are the nerve and life of the cities, and are the industries of which the plebs eat.[180] They also keep military exercises in order, and have many ordinances to make sure they do.

Therefore, a prince, who has a strong city and who does not make himself hated, cannot be attacked and, though he be, whoever attacks him will come away from it with shame; because the things of the world are so changeable that it is impossible to keep armies slothfully besieging him for a year. And whoever might reply: If the people have their possessions outside and see them burn, they will not stand it, and the long siege and the care for one's own will make them forget the prince: I answer that a powerful and spirited prince will always overcome all these difficulties, now giving the subjects hope that the evil not be long, now fear of the enemy's cruelty, now with dexterity making sure of those who appear to him too fiery.

Beyond this, the enemy, reasonably, must[181] burn and ruin the country upon his arrival, while the spirits of men are still hot and willing for defense; and because of this the prince needs fear[182] the less, since by the time a few days have passed and spirits have cooled, the damages have already been done and the hurts[183] received, and there is no more remedy; and then they come together with their prince all the more, it seeming that he has an obligation to them because their houses have been burned, and their possessions ruined, for his defense. And the nature of men is, to oblige oneself because of the benefits one gives, as well as because of those one receives. Therefore, if one will well consider everything, it be not difficult for a prudent prince to keep the spirits of the citizens firm during the beginning of a siege and later, so long as they lack not the means of living or of defending themselves.

178. *Conveniente*, "as is convenient."

179. *Pasciuta*, the state of a sheep after it has grazed.

180. *Pasca*, subjunctive of the verb *pascere*, which refers primarily to animals.

181. Subjunctive, i.e., should be expected to burn and ruin.

182. *Dubitare*, "doubt."

183. *Mali*, "evils."

XI

De principatibus ecclesiasticis
(Of ecclesiastical principalities)

It only remains to us at present to reason of ecclesiastical principalities: all difficulties concerning which come before they are possessed: because, though they are acquired either by virtue or by fortune, they are kept without either because they are upheld by orders grown ancient in religion,[184] which have been so powerful and of such quality that they keep their princes in state regardless of how they proceed and live. Only these have states, and they do not defend them; subjects, and they do not govern them: and the states are not taken from them, though undefended, and the subjects, though not governed, do not concern themselves about it, neither do they think about, nor can they estrange themselves from them. Therefore, only these principalities are secure and happy. But since they are upheld by superior cause, to which the human mind does not reach, I will leave off speaking of them; because, since they are exalted and maintained by God, discussing them would be the doing of a presumptuous and daring[185] man. Nonetheless, if someone were to inquire of me why the Church has come to such greatness in the temporal, so that before Alexander[186] the Italian powers, and not *solum*[187] those who were called powers, but each baron and lord, though small, esteemed it little in the temporal, and now a king of France trembles at him, and the Church has been able to pull him out of Italy, and to ruin the Venetians: it does not seem superfluous to commit the matter to memory[188] in good part, though it be well known. Before Charles, king of France, had passed into Italy,[189] this province was under the power[190] of the

184. *ordini antiquati nella religione.* "Orders" are either "aged" or "grown ancient" or "grown ancient and out of fashion" in religion.

185. *Temerario*, one who acts with temerity. Since Machiavelli proceeds to discuss precisely this subject, the adjectives apply to him.

186. Pope Alexander VI Borgia.

187. Latin *non solum*, not only. Here begins another run of mock solemnities.

188. That is, to learn it by heart.

189. In 1494.

190. *Imperio*, literally, "empire." By the use of the word *empire*, Machiavelli obviously contrasted the power of the pope and other petty emperors with the power of the

pope, the Venetians, the king of Naples, the duke of Milan, and the Florentines. These powers had to have two principal concerns: the one, that a
foreigner not enter into Italy with arms; the other, that each of them might
occupy more state. Those who concerned them the most were the pope and
the Venetians. And the unity of all the others was needed to hold back the
Venetians, as it was in the defense of Ferrara; and to keep down the pope
they[191] used the barons of Rome, among whom there was always cause for
trouble,[192] since they were divided into two factions, Orsini and Colonnesi,
and, standing with arms in hand and eyes upon the pope, they kept the
papacy weak and unsteady. And though once in a while a spirited pope, as
was Sixtus,[193] might arise, *tamen*[194] neither fortune nor wisdom could ever
free him from these discomforts. And the brevity of their life was the cause
of it; because, in the ten years a pope lived on average, he could hardly
lower one of the factions; and if, for instance, one [pope] had almost extinguished the Colonnesi, another one hostile to the Orsini would arise, who
would make them[195] rise again, and he did not have time[196] to extinguish the
Orsini. This made the temporal forces of the pope little esteemed in Italy.
Then Alexander VI arose, who, of all the popes who had ever been, showed
how much a pope could prevail with money and with forces. And through
the instrumentality of Duke Valentino and because of the coming of the
French, he did all those things which I said above concerning the actions of
the duke. And even though it was not his intention to make the Church great,
nonetheless, what the duke did redounded to the greatness of the Church;
which after his death, once the duke had died, was the heir of his toils. Then
came Pope Julius, who found the Church great, having all of Romagna, and,
because of Alexander's threshings, the barons of Rome had been snuffed
out and their factions annihilated; moreover, he found the door still open
to a way of accumulating money, never[197] used before Alexander, which

---

Holy Roman Empire, of which Italy was supposed to be a province. This confusion of the
roles of pope and emperor is another small way by which Machiavelli seeks to discredit
the premises of medieval politics.

191. Presumably, the powers.

192. *Scandolo*, literally, "scandal." There was plenty of that, too.

193. Sixtus IV.

194. Latin, "nevertheless."

195. The Colonnesi.

196. *A tempo*, i.e., he could not do it in time.

197. "*Non mai piu usitato da Alessandro indietro.*" This jumbled phrase uses a

things Julius not *solum*[198] continued but increased; he thought to gain Bologna for himself, to extinguish the Venetians, and to chase the French from Italy; and all these enterprises succeeded for him, and with so much more credit for himself, insomuch as he did everything to increase the Church and not any private man. He also kept the Orsini and the Colonnesi parties within the limits in which he found them; and, even though some chiefs among them might have been able to make trouble, *tamen*[199] two things stopped them: one, the greatness of the Church, which dismayed them; the other, not having their own cardinals, who are the origins of tumults among them. Nor will these parties ever remain quiet so long as they have cardinals; because having them nourishes parties, within Rome and outside it, and those barons are forced to defend them: and thus the discord and tumults among barons springs from the ambitions of prelates. Therefore, the holiness of Pope Leo[200] found the papacy most powerful: which is why one hopes that if the others made it great with arms, this one will make it most great and venerable with his goodness and his infinite other virtues.[201]

---

future-oriented term to refer to the past. *Mai piu* means "never more," connoting that the deed had not been done previously. But *non mai piu usitato* can also mean "never been used." Since the subject is the Church's self-enrichment through the sale of indulgences, a subject that five years after the writing of *The Prince*, in 1517, fueled the Protestant Reformation, Machiavelli is beating a wide, fuzzy circle around the hottest of bushes. And then he moves on quickly.

198. Latin *non solum*, "not only." The reference is solemnly broadened to the kinds of things done by Cesare Borgia.

199. Latin, "nevertheless."

200. Leo X Medici, son of Lorenzo. Machiavelli does not say His Holiness, pointedly referring not so much to Leo as to Leo's titular holiness, as he had referred to his father's titular majesty.

201. Cf. Machiavelli's reference in Chap. XVII to the "infinite virtues" and to the "*other* virtues" (emphasis added) of Hannibal. The only one of Hannibal's qualities he mentions is "inhuman cruelty." Machiavelli has no illusions about the Medicis.

XII

Quot sint genera militiae et de mercenariis militibus
(How many are the kinds of militia, and of mercenary soldiers)

Having discussed in particular all the qualities of the principalities which I proposed to discuss at the beginning, and in some part [202] considered the causes of their being good and evil,[203] and shown the ways[204] by which many have tried to acquire them and keep them, it now remains to me generally to discuss the offenses and defenses that can occur in each of the aforenamed. We have said above that it is necessary to a prince to have good foundations for himself; otherwise he necessarily comes to ruin.[205] And the principal foundations that all states have,[206] new ones like old or mixed ones, are good laws and good arms. And because there cannot be good laws where there are not good arms, and where there are good arms there must be good laws, I will leave aside reasoning of laws and will speak of arms.

I say, therefore, that the arms with which a prince defends his state either are his own or they are mercenary, either auxiliary or mixed. The mercenary and auxiliary are useless and dangerous; and if one holds his state on the basis of mercenary arms, he will never be firm or secure; because they are disunited, ambitious, without discipline, unfaithful; gallant among friends, vile among enemies; no fear of God, no faith with men; and one defers ruin insofar as one defers the attack; and in peace you are despoiled by them, in

---

202. *Qualche parte* also means "somewhere."

203. "*Del bene e del male esseri loro*," "of their well-being and of their being sick." Machiavelli quietly introduces the confusion between good and political effectiveness on one hand, and evil and political ineffectiveness on the other. This will shortly become the very center of the book.

204. *Modi*, "modes."

205. *Conviene.* If he does not have good foundations, he will come to ruin *necessarily.*

206. Subjunctive, i.e., the foundations that states *may* have. Machiavelli is stating his definite view as if it were tentative.

war by the enemy. The cause of this is that they have no other love nor other cause to keep them in camp but a little pay, which is not sufficient to make them want to die for you. They want to be your soldiers while you do not make war; but when war comes they want either to flee or to go away. I should take little toil to persuade on this point, because nowadays the ruin of Italy is caused by nothing else than by having reposed[207] upon mercenary arms for many years. These arms had gained some advantages for some, and appeared gallant among themselves; but when the foreigner came, they showed what they were. Hence, Charles, king of France, was allowed[208] to take Italy with chalk; and he who said that our sins were the cause of it,[209] said the truth; but it was not quite the ones which he believed, but those of which I have spoken: and because these were sins of princes, even they suffered the penalty.

I want better to demonstrate the nefariousness of these arms. The mercenary captains are either excellent men or not: if they are, you cannot trust them, because they will always aspire to their own greatness, either by oppressing you who are their boss, or by oppressing others outside of your intention; but if he is not virtuous, he ruins you by the ordinary.[210] And if one answers that whoever has arms in his hand will do this, whether mercenary or not, I would reply that arms are used by either a prince or a republic. The prince must go in person and himself do the office of captain; the republic has to send its citizens: and when they send a man who does not turn out to be worthy, it must change him; and when he does succeed, to bind him with laws so that he might not overstep the mark. And by experience one sees that only princes and armed republics make very great progress, and that mercenary arms never do anything but damage. And a republic armed with its own army comes to the obedience[211] of one of its own citizens with greater difficulty than one armed with foreign arms.

Rome and Sparta were armed and free for many centuries. The Swiss are

207. *Riposatasi.* The meaning is that Italy had counted on mercenary armies to the point that these armies had become the foundation on which Italian politics rested. But the word *riposatasi* conveys the image of a country that had laid down for a lazy rest, and implies that these armies were the bed on which the country rested.

208. *lui licito*, "it was licit [to King Charles]." Chalk was used to mark the houses to be used as lodging for the King's soldiers.

209. Girolamo Savonarola, in a sermon in November 1494.

210. That is, by ordinary, routine incompetence.

211. That is, a republic that has its own army succumbs to a homegrown dictator more rarely than one that hires mercenaries.

most armed and most free. Among ancient mercenary armies *in exemplis*[212] are the Carthaginians; who were about to be[213] oppressed by their own mercenaries after the first war with the Romans, even though the Carthaginians had their own citizens as chiefs. Philip of Macedon, after the death of Epaminondas, was made captain of their people;[214] and after their victory took their liberty from them. The Milanese, Duke Filippo having died, hired[215] Francesco Sforza against the Venetians; who, having overcome the enemies at Caravaggio, joined with them to oppress his Milanese employers. Sforza the father, having been hired[216] by Queen Giovanna of Naples, left her disarmed all of a sudden, because of which she was constrained to throw herself into the lap of the king of Aragon in order not to lose her kingdom. And if the Venetians and the Florentines have somehow increased their empire with these armies, and their captains did not make themselves princes through them but defended them, I answer that the Florentines in this case were favored by chance; because among the virtuous captains, whom they could have feared, some did not win, some found opposition, others turned their ambition elsewhere. The one who did not win was Giovanni Aucut,[217] whose faith one could not know because he had not won; but everyone will confess that if they had won, the Florentines would have been at his discretion. Sforza always had the Bracceschi against him, so that each guarded the other: Francesco turned his attention to Lombardy; Braccio against the Church and the Kingdom of Naples. But let us come to what happened a short time ago. The Florentines made Paolo Vitelli their captain, a most prudent man, who from private status had taken on a very great reputation. If this one had taken Pisa, no one could deny that it would have been necessary[218] for the Florentines to stay with him; because if he had become their enemies' soldier,[219] they had no remedy; and if they had kept him, they would have had to obey him.

If one will consider the progresses of the Venetians, one will see that they operated securely and gloriously while they made war themselves:

212. Latin, "for example."

213. *Furono per essere*, "were to be," i.e., in the First Punic War, 241–237 B.C.

214. 346 B.C.

215. *Soldarono* (third pers. pl. of the verb *soldare*), meaning "engaged for *soldi*," i.e., money. Filippo Visconti died in 1448.

216. *Soldato*, the noun *soldier*, is also the past participle of the verb *soldare*.

217. Sir John Hawkwood.

218. *Conveniva*, "it would have been convenient," and therefore necessary.

219. *Soldato*, i.e., hireling.

which was before they turned to enterprises on land: where they operated most virtuously with their own gentlemen and with the armed plebs; but as they began to fight on land, they left that virtue and followed the customs of Italy. And at the beginning of their expansion on land they did not have to fear much from their captains, not having been there much and being of great reputation; but as they became bigger, which was under Carmignola, they had a taste of this mistake. Because, having seen him most virtuous, having beaten the duke of Milan under his government, and knowing on the other hand how he cooled toward[220] war, they judged that they could no longer win with him, because he did not want to, nor could they fire him lest they lose again what they had conquered; which is why they were constrained by necessity to kill him in order to make sure of him. Thereafter they had as their captains Bartolommeo da Bergamo, Roberto da San Severino, the count of Pitigliano, and similar ones; with whom they had to fear their losses, not their gains: as occurred then at Vailá, where in one day they lost that which they had acquired in eight hundred years with such toil. Because these arms generate only slow, late, and weak acquisitions, and sudden and miraculous losses. And because I have come with these examples[221] in Italy, which has been governed for many years by mercenary arms, I want to discuss them more from the top,[222] so that, having seen their origin and progression, one might better correct them.

You have to perceive[223] that, as soon as in these latter times the empire began to be thrown back from Italy and the pope took greater reputation in its temporal affairs, Italy divided itself into several states; because many of the big cities took up arms against their nobles, who earlier had oppressed them with the emperor's support, and the Church [took up arms against] the cities[224] in order to give itself temporal reputation; in many others their own citizens became princes. Hence it is that, Italy having come almost into the hands of the Church and of some republics, and those priests and those other citizens not being used to practicing arms, they began to hire for-

220. Francesco da Carmignola led Venice to victory at Maclodio in 1427 but lost his ardor for the war.

221. I.e., "because I have written of these Italian examples."

222. I.e., "from the beginning," but also "from on high," that is, "I want to treat the whole matter systematically."

223. Plural you, followed by the verb *intendere*. The sense is that of the colloquial English expression, "You've got to get this into your head."

224. I.e., the Church took up arms against the cities. But Machiavelli chooses not to say it clearly.

eigners. The first who gave reputation to this militia[225] was Alberigo da Conio of Romagna. From his model[226] descended, among others, Braccio and Sforza, who were the arbiters of Italy in their time. After these came all the others who have governed these armies until our times. And the consequence of their virtue has been that Italy has been run over by Charles, preyed upon by Louis, raped by Fernando,[227] and vilified by the Swiss. The order[228] to which they have adhered has been, first, to give reputation to themselves, to take reputation away from the infantries.[229] They did this because, being without a state and in business, having few infantrymen would not give them reputations and many they could not feed; and therefore they limited themselves to cavalry, where with a supportable number they were fed and honored. And in the end things came to the point that in an army of twenty thousand soldiers two thousand infantrymen were not to be found. Beyond this, they had used every effort[230] to take away from themselves and from the soldiers the toil and the fear, not killing each other in fights, but taking one another prisoner and without ransom. They did not run to attack the cities at night; while those in the cities did not run to attack the tents; they did not make either a palisade or moat around the camp; they did not campaign in winter. And all these things were permitted in their military orders, and invented by them in order to avoid, as is said, both toil and dangers: so much that they have led[231] Italy to be slave and vilified.

225. I.e., to this way of doing things military.

226. *Disciplina*, "discipline."

227. Ferdinand the Catholic, king of Spain.

228. I.e., the priorities.

229. The infantries are the forces raised among the local citizens.

230. *Industria*. The same word was used in the previous sentence, where it was translated as "business."

231. *Condotta*, as in *condottiere*, mercenary captain. I.e., the mercenary leaders and captains have led and captained Italy into slavery.

XIII

De militibus auxiliaris, mixtis et propriis
(Of auxiliary soldiery, mixed and one's own)

Auxiliary arms, which are the other useless arms, are when a powerful one is called to come help and defend you with his arms: as in recent times Pope Julius, having seen the sad proof of his mercenary armies in the Ferrara enterprise, turned to auxiliaries; and contracted[232] with Ferdinand, king of Spain, to help him with his people and armies. These armies can be useful and good for themselves, but they are almost always harmful to him who calls on them; because, losing, you remain undone; winning, you remain their prisoner. *Et*[233] though the ancient histories be full of these examples, nonetheless I do not want to leave out this fresh example of Pope Julius II; whose decision[234] to stick himself wholly into the hands of a foreigner because he wanted Ferrara could not have been less thought out. But his good fortune spawned a third thing, so that he did not reap the fruit of his bad choice:[235] because, after his auxiliaries had broken at Ravenna, the Swiss rose up and chased out the victors, outside of any expectation of his own and of others. He did not remain a prisoner of the enemy, because they had fled, nor of his auxiliaries, since he had won with arms other than theirs. The Florentines, being wholly disarmed, led[236] ten thousand Frenchmen to Pisa to take it: because of which decision they incurred more danger than at any time in their travails. The emperor of Constantinople, to oppose his

232. *Convenne*, from the verb *convenire*, "to convene," "to make a *convenzione*" (convention or contract). Given Machiavelli's frequent equation of *convenire* with both convenience and necessity, he characterizes the pope's deal with the king of Spain as a convenient deal.

233. Latin, "and." Again, solemnity.

234. *Partito del quale*, "whose chosen part."

235. *Elezione*, "election." Popes, of course, have elections in two senses: they are elected, and they elect. Julius chose badly and, Machiavelli hints broadly, was badly chosen.

236. *Conclussone*, i.e., they engaged or hired. This awkward expression is probably a pun on *condussone*, "they led [a certain number] of them."

neighbors, put ten thousand Turks into Greece; who did not want to leave after the war ended: which was the beginning of Greece's servitude to the infidels.

Therefore, whoever wants to be unable to win, let him avail himself of such armies, because they are much more dangerous than the mercenary ones: because with these ruin is accomplished; they are all united, all committed to obeying others: but the mercenary ones, once they have won, need more time and greater occasion to hurt you, since they are not all of one body, and, having been found and paid by you, and in which one-third may be commanded by you, cannot swiftly take up so much authority as to hurt you. In sum, in mercenary ones, indolence is more dangerous, while in the auxiliaries, virtue is.

Therefore, a wise prince has always fled these arms and turned to his own; and has sooner wanted to lose with his than to win with others', judging a victory that is acquired with alien arms not a true one. I will never fear[237] to cite Cesare Borgia and his actions. The duke entered Romagna with auxiliary arms, leading wholly French troops, and with these he took Imola and Forlì. But, such arms not seeming secure to him, he turned to the mercenary ones, judging that there be less danger in them, and engaged both the Orsini and the Vitelli. Later, managing and finding them doubtful, unfaithful, and dangerous, he extinguished them and turned to his own. And one can easily see the difference between these arms, considering the difference between the duke's reputation, when he had only the French and when he had Orsini and Vitelli, and when he was left with his own soldiers and on his own: and always one will find it increased; never was he so esteemed as when everyone saw that he was the total owner of his arms.

I did not want to depart from examples both Italian and fresh: *tamen*[238] I do not want to leave out Hiero of Syracuse, since he was among those previously mentioned by me. This one, as I said, having been made chief of the armies of the Syracusans, right away recognized that mercenary militia are not useful, because the *condottieri* are made like our Italians;[239] and, it seeming to him that he was unable to keep them or to let them go, he had them all cut to pieces: and thereafter made war with his own arms and not with alien ones. I yet want to commit to memory one scene from the Old

237. Literally, "I will never doubt to allege."

238. Latin, "nevertheless."

239. I.e., all *condottieri* anywhere, anytime, are made of the same stuff as the Italian *condottieri* of Machiavelli's time. In the subsequent sentences, note Machiavelli's constant pairing of bloody tyrants with men whom the Bible describes as instruments of God.

Testament for this purpose. When David offered himself to Saul to go fight with the Philistine challenger Goliath, Saul, to give him spirit, armed him with his arms: which David, as soon as he had put them on, refused, saying that with them he could not make use of himself well, and therefore that he wanted to meet the enemy with his sling and his knife.

In the end, the arms of others either fall off you, or weigh you down, or squeeze you. Charles VII, father of King Louis XI, having liberated France from the English with his fortune and virtue, recognized this necessity to arm oneself with one's own arms, and ordained in his kingdom the ordinance of the men-at-arms and of the infantries.[240] Thereafter King Louis, his son, extinguished that of the infantry and began to hire the Swiss: which error, followed by the others, is, as is now evident in fact, the cause of that kingdom's dangers. Because, having given reputation to the Swiss, he has reviled all his armies; because he has extinguished his infantries and has obligated his men-at-arms to the arms of others; because, being habituated to fight[241] alongside the Swiss, they do not think they can win without them. From which it follows that the French do not suffice against the Swiss, and that without the Swiss they do not try against others. Therefore, the French armies have been mixed, part mercenary and part their own: which arms all together are much better than the simply auxiliary or simply mercenary, and much inferior to one's own. And let the said example suffice; because if Charles's ordinance were increased or preserved, the kingdom of France would be unsurpassable. But the small prudence of men begins something which, because it tastes good then, one does not become aware of the poison under it: as I said above of the Aetolian fever.

Therefore, whoever in a principality does not recognize evils when they are born, is not truly wise: and this is given to few. And if one were to consider the beginning of the Roman Empire's ruin, one will find it to have started in the hiring of the Goths; because from that beginning they began to enervate the forces of the Roman Empire; and all that virtue that was taken from it was given to them. I therefore conclude that no principality is secure without having its own arms; on the contrary, it is wholly obligated to

240. King Charles VII is the father of the French army and the victor in the Hundred Years' War, which ended in 1453. The nine thousand horsemen of the "*compagnies d'ordonnance,*" which he formally established in 1435–36, depended solely on him, were the primary instrument by which he built the centralized, modern, French state, and are the model of all subsequent standing armies in Western civilization.

241. *Assuefatte a militare,* used in the sense of "broken" to do military things, as a horse is "broken" to be ridden.

fortune, not having virtue to defend it in adversity. And it was always the opinion and motto of wise men: "There is nothing more unstable in human things than fame or power not upheld by its own force." And one's own arms are those which are composed either of subjects or of citizens or of your creatures: all the others are either mercenary or auxiliary. And the way[242] to ordain one's own arms will be easy to find, if one will discuss the orders of the four[243] mentioned above by me,[244] and if one will see how Philip, father of Alexander the Great, and how many republics and princes have armed and ordered themselves: upon which orders I wholly base myself.

242. *Modo*, "mode."

243. The verb *discorrere* also means "to run over" in the sense of "to examine."

244. Charles VII, Hiero of Syracuse, David, and Cesare Borgia.

XIV

Quod principem deceat circa militiam
(What might pertain to a prince concerning the military)

Therefore, a prince must not have any objective nor any thought, nor take up any art, other than the art of war and its ordering and discipline; because it is the only art that pertains to him who commands. And it is of such virtue that not only does it maintain those who were born princes, but many times makes men rise to that rank from private station;[245] and conversely one sees that when princes have thought more of delicacies than of arms, they have lost their state. And the first cause that makes you lose it is to neglect this art; and the cause that makes you acquire it is to be proficient[246] in this art; Francesco Sforza became duke of Milan from private individual because he was armed. His children became private individuals[247] from dukes because they fled the discomforts of arms. Because among the causes[248] of evil which being unarmed brings you, it makes you contemptible,[249] which is one of those infamies against which the prince must guard himself, as will be said below. Because there is no proportion whatever between one who is armed and one who is unarmed: and it is not reasonable that he who is armed willingly obey him who is unarmed, and that the unarmed remain secure among armed servants. Because, there being disdain in the one and suspicion in the others, it is not possible that they work well together. And because of this, a prince who is not expert in military things, beyond other griefs, as is said, cannot be esteemed by his soldiers, nor trust them.

Consequently, he must never lift his thoughts from the exercise of war: which he can do in two ways: the one with works, and the other with the

---

245. *Fortuna,* "fortune," here meaning station or rank. One's rank or state at birth is a matter of *fortuna.*

246. *Professo,* literally, "to be a professor" — a proficient one.

247. Ludovico (II Moro), ousted by Louis XII in 1500, and perhaps Massimiliano, who reconquered the city in 1512 and lost it again in 1515.

248. *Cagioni,* also "occasions," "reasons."

249. I.e., worthy of being held in contempt.

mind. And as for works, beyond keeping his own[250] well ordered and exercised, he must always stay out on hunts, and through these inure his body to hardships, and meanwhile learn the nature of sites and come to know how the mountains rise, how the valleys open, how the plains lie, and to perceive the nature of the rivers and of the swamps, and to put the greatest care into this. Which knowledge is useful in two ways. First, one learns to know one's country and can better perceive its defenses; moreover, through knowledge and experience of those sites, [one learns] to understand with ease any other site which it might be necessary for him to think of at another time: because the hilltops, the valleys, the plains, the rivers, the swamps that are in Tuscany, for example, have certain similarities with those of the other provinces: so that from the knowledge of one province one can easily come to the knowledge of the others. And that prince who lacks this expertise[251] lacks the first quality that a captain needs to have; because this [art] teaches how to find the enemy, how to pick quarters, to lead armies, to arrange battles, to besiege lands to your advantage. Among the other praises which have been given to Philopoemen, prince of the Acheans, by the writers is that in times of peace he never thought of anything but of the ways[252] of war; and when he was in the country with friends, he often stopped and reasoned with them — If the enemy were upon that hill, and we found ourselves here with our army, which of us would have the advantage? How could one, keeping good order, go to meet them? If we wanted to retreat, how would we have to do it? If they were to retreat, how could we pursue them? — and he proposed to them, as they traveled, all the cases which can arise in an army; heard[253] their opinion, spoke his, corroborated it with reasons: so that by means of these continuous cogitations no accident could ever spring up in the leading of armies, for which he did not have[254] the remedy.

But for the exercise of the mind, the prince must read the histories, and in those consider the actions of excellent men, see how they have carried[255] themselves in the wars, examine the causes of their victory and losses, to be

250. Presumably troops, but not limited to these, implicitly including all those who are "his own."

251. *Perizie* (pl.).

252. *Modi.*

253. *Intendeva*, "perceived." Here the meaning is "listened to."

254. Subjunctive. Machiavelli makes no guarantees.

255. *Governati*, "governed."

able to avoid the latter and imitate the former; and above all to do as some excellent man has done in the past, who took up imitating someone before his time who had been lauded and glorified, and always kept his deeds[256] and actions close to him: as is said that Alexander the Great imitated Achilles, Caesar Alexander, Scipio Cyrus. And whoever reads the life of Cyrus written by Xenophon thereafter recognizes in the life of Scipio how much that imitation was his glory and to what extent Scipio conformed[257] himself in chastity, affability, humaneness, liberality to those things which were written of Cyrus by Xenophon. A wise prince must imitate these similar modes and never in peaceful times remain lazy, but capitalize on it with industry, in order to be able to use it in adversity, so that, when fortune changes, it might find him prepared to resist her.

256. *Gesti*, "gestures."
257. Subjunctive, because, of course, he conformed very little.

XV

De his rebus quibus homines et praesertim principes laudantur aut vituperantur
(Of those things for which men, and especially princes, are lauded or vilified)

It now remains to see what the modes and rules[258] of a prince should be with subjects or with friends. And because I know that many have written of this, I fear[259] being held presumptuous for writing of it again, especially since in arguing this matter I depart from the orders of others. But, it being my intention to write something useful to him who perceives[260] it, it has appeared to me more convenient to go after the effective truth of the thing rather than the imagination of it.[261] And many have imagined for themselves republics and principalities that no one has ever seen or known to be in reality. Because how one ought to live is so far removed from how one lives that he who lets go of what is done for that which one ought to do sooner learns ruin than his own preservation: because a man who might want to make a show[262] of goodness in all things necessarily[263] comes to ruin among so many who are not good. Because of this it is necessary to a prince, wanting to maintain himself, to learn how to be able to be not good and to use this and not use it according to necessity.

Therefore, leaving behind the things imagined about a prince, and discussing those which are true, I say that all men, when they are spoken of, and especially the princes, because they are placed higher, are noted for some of

258. *Modi e governi*, "modes and governments."

259. *Dubito*, "I doubt."

260. *Intende*. Note that Machiavelli does not say "a chi se ne intende," i.e., "to him who knows what he is doing." Nor does he say he wants to "dare da intendere," i.e., to put something over on the reader. Rather, he will speak straight to whomever is able to follow him.

261. I.e., than to go after that which is imagined of it.

262. *Professione*, "profession."

263. *Conviene*, it is convenient or necessary, or, by the operation of conventional society, he will come to ruin.

these qualities which bring them blame or praise. And some are held to be liberal, some miserly (using a Tuscan term, because an *avaro* in our language is still one who desires to have by rapine; we call him *misero* who excessively abstains from using his own); someone is considered a giver, someone rapacious; someone cruel, someone piteous; someone fickle, another faithful; someone effeminate and pusillanimous, the other fierce and spirited; someone humane, the other haughty; someone lascivious, the other chaste; someone simple, the other astute; someone hard, the other easy; someone grave, the other lighthearted; someone religious, the other unbelieving and such. And I know that everyone will confess that it would be a most laudable thing that a prince find in himself, of all the above-written qualities, those which are thought to be good: but because he cannot have them, nor wholly observe them, because of the human conditions which do not permit, it is necessary for him to be so prudent as to know how to avoid the infamy of those[264] which would take the state from him, and to guard himself against those that might not take it from him, if it is possible; but, it not being possible, one can let them go with less fear.[265] *Et etiam*[266] let him not care about incurring infamy for those vices without which he might hardly save the state; because, if one considers everything well, one will find that something that appears a virtue, if followed, would be his ruin, and that some other thing that appears a vice, if followed, results in his security and well-being.[267]

264. I.e., those qualities which, because of their effect on one's own *stato*, are most truly bad by Machiavelli's definition.

265. *Rispetto*, i.e., one need care less about these qualities.

266. Latin, "and also."

267. *Bene essere. Il bene* means "the good." *Bene essere* implies "being good" in addition to "being well."

XVI
De liberalitate et parsimonia
(Of liberality and parsimony)

Therefore, starting off at the first of the above-written qualities, I say that it would be well to be considered liberal: nonetheless, liberality, used so that you may be so considered, hurts you; because, if it is used virtuously and as it should be used, it would not be known and you will not shed the infamy of its opposite. And consequently, if you want to maintain the name of liberal among men, it is necessary not to spare any sumptuousness; so that, always, a prince who does this will consume all his resources in such works; and in the end, if he wants to retain the name of liberal, he will be required to weigh down the people extraordinarily and to be taxy[268] and to do all the things that can be done to have money. This will begin to make him hateful to the subjects and little esteemed by anyone, since this makes him poor; so that, having hurt the many and rewarded the few with this liberality of his, he feels[269] every least unrest and is imperiled by the first danger that comes along: when he realizes this and wants to pull back from it,[270] he right away incurs the infamy of the miser. Therefore, since a prince cannot use this virtue of liberality without damage to himself, if he is prudent he must not worry about the reputation of miser: because with time he will be considered even more liberal, when it is seen that because of his parsimony his income suffices him, that he can defend himself against whomever makes war on him, and that he can undertake enterprises without weighing down the peoples; by which token he comes to use liberality toward all those from whom he does not take, who are infinite, and miserliness toward all to whom he does not give, who are few. In our times we have not seen great things done if not by those who have been held to be misers: the others having been extinguished. Pope Julius II, though he had used a reputation for liberality to reach the papacy, did not think to keep it later, in order to enable himself to make war. The present king of France has made many wars without placing an extraordinary tariff on his own, because his long-

---

268. *Essere fiscale*, i.e., to tax a lot. Machiavelli makes a lively adjective out of the verb "to be" and a word meaning "pertaining to taxes."

269. *Sente*, i.e., is vulnerable to.

270. The situation created by his liberality.

time parsimony provided for the extraordinary expenses. And the present king of Spain, if he were considered liberal, would not have undertaken or won so many enterprises.

Consequently, a prince must care little about incurring the name of miser in order not to have to rob the subjects, to be able to defend himself, not to become poor and contemptible, not to be forced to become rapacious; because this is one of those vices that allow him to reign. And if anyone were to say: Caesar achieved empire with liberality, and many others have come to the highest ranks because of having been and having been considered liberal, I answer: Either you are already a prince, or you are on the way to acquiring it. In the first case, this liberality is damaging: in the second, it is indeed[271] necessary to be considered liberal. And Caesar was one of those who wanted to come to the principality of Rome; but if once he had come, he had survived and had not tempered those expenses, he would have destroyed that empire.[272] And if one were to reply: Many who have been considered most liberal have been princes, and have done great things with armies: I answer you: either the prince spends from his own and his subjects', or from others'. In the first case he must be stingy; in the other he must not neglect any kind of liberality. And for that prince who goes out with armies, who feeds on prey, booty, and taxes and manages others' goods, this liberality is necessary to him, otherwise he would not be followed by the soldiers. And one can be a larger donor of what is not yours or your subjects'; as were Cyrus, Caesar, and Alexander; because spending that which is yours harms you. And nothing consumes itself like liberality; for while you use it you lose the capacity to use it; and you become either poor and contemptible or, to dodge poverty, rapacious and odious. And among all the things against which a prince must guard himself is being contemptible and odious; and liberality leads you to both. Therefore, there is more wisdom in keeping for oneself the name of the miser, which brings forth infamy without hatred, than to be required to incur the name of rapacious because you want the name liberal, which brings forth infamy with hatred.

271. *Bene necessario*, or "good 'n' necessary." Here goodness and necessity are coupled, as goodness and "doing well" were previously.

272. *Impero* here means both his own power and the empire over which he held power.

XVII

De crudelitate et pietate, et an sit melius amari quam timeri, vel e contra
(Of cruelty and pity; and whether it is better to be loved than feared, or the contrary)

Descending next to the other previously alleged qualities, I say that each prince must desire to be considered merciful and not cruel. Nonetheless, he must be wary not to use this mercy badly. Cesare Borgia was considered cruel; nonetheless, that cruelty of his had fixed up Romagna, united it, reduced it to peace and reliability. Which, if it were to be well considered, would be seen to have been much more merciful than the Florentine people, which, in order to escape the name of cruel, let Pistoia be destroyed. Consequently, a prince must not care about the infamy of cruelty in order to keep his subjects united and faithful;[273] because with very few examples he will be more merciful than those who, because of too much mercy, allow disorders to go on, from which spring killings or depredations: because these normally offend a whole collectivity, while those executions which come from the prince offend an individual. And among all princes, it is impossible for the new prince to escape the name of cruel, since new states are full of dangers. And Vergil says in Dido's mouth:

> *Res dura, et regni novitas me talia cogunt moliri,*
> *et late fines custode tueri.*
> (Hard things and the newness of the reign constrain me to use
> such methods and to defend the borders with vast guard.)

Nonetheless, he must be slow[274] to believe and to move, neither making himself the object of fear, and to proceed in a moderate way, with prudence

273. *Fede*, "faith," here means "reliable." Machiavelli is certainly not talking about forcing citizens to keep the Catholic faith.

274. *Grave*, implying deliberateness and consciousness of consequences at least as much as lack of speed.

and humaneness, so that too much confidence not make him careless and too much diffidence not render him intolerable.

From this springs a dispute: whether it is better to be loved than feared or the reverse. It is answered that one would want to be both; but, because it is difficult to force[275] them together whenever one has to do without either of the two, it is much more secure to be feared than to be loved. Because this can generally be said about men: that they are ungrateful, fickle, dissimulators, apt to flee peril, covetous of gain; and while you do them good, they are all yours, they offer you their blood, their things, their life, their children, as I said above, when need is far off; but when it draws near to you, they revolt. And that prince who bases himself entirely on their words, finding himself naked of other preparations, falls to ruin; because the friendships which a prince obtains for a price, and not by greatness and nobility of spirit, are merited, but they are not had and cannot be spent in time.[276] And men are less reticent[277] to offend one who makes himself loved than one who makes himself feared; because love is held by a bond of obligation which, since men are shabby, is broken for their own utility upon every occasion; but timorousness is secured by fear of punishment which never lets you go. Nonetheless, the prince must make himself feared in such a way that, if he does not obtain love, he may escape hatred; because being feared and not hated can go together very well; which he will do always when he keeps[278] himself from his citizens' and his subjects' possessions, and from their women: and even when he might have need to proceed against someone's blood,[279] he should do it when there might be convenient[280] justification and manifest cause; but, above all, [he should] abstain from other people's things; because men sooner forget the death of the father than they do the loss of patrimony.[281] Moreover, causes for taking away things are never lacking; and he who begins to live by depradation

275. *Accozzare* has two separate meanings: striking together and mingling forcefully.

276. Here, time means "at an opportune moment," "at crucial times," or "when you need them."

277. The word *rispetto* is used to imply not so much the cause as the effect of a respectful attitude.

278. Subjunctive.

279. *Sangue* can mean life or blood relations.

280. The word *conveniente* here means both meet or pertinent (i.e., rightful) and merely convenient.

281. Patrimony is the legacy of *patres*, fathers. The following sentence is elliptical.

always finds cause to take that which belongs to others; and, on the contrary, against [human] blood the [causes to proceed] are rarer and disappear sooner.

But when the prince is with armies and rules multitudes of soldiers, then it is entirely necessary not to care about the name of cruel; because without this name an army was never united, nor disposed to any deed of arms. Among Hannibal's admirable actions is numbered this, that although he had a very large army made up of infinite kinds of men, led to fight in alien lands, there never arose any dissension, neither among them nor against the prince, in his bad fortune as in good. Which could not arise from anything other than that inhuman cruelty of his, which, together with his infinite virtues, always made him venerable and terrible in the regard of his soldiers; and without it[282] his other[283] virtues would not have sufficed him to produce that effect. And writers of little consideration on the one hand admire this action of his, on the other damn its principal cause. And that it be true that his other virtues would not have sufficed, one can see from Scipio, most rare not only in his times but in memory of things known, whose armies in Spain rebelled against him. Which sprang from nothing other than his excessive mercy, which had given his soldiers more license than was meet[284] for military discipline. This was reproved in the Senate by Fabius Maximus, who called him corrupter of the Roman militia. The Locrians, having been destroyed by a delegate of Scipio, were not avenged by him, nor was the insolence of that legate corrected, all springing from that easy nature of his; to the point that someone in the Senate who wanted to excuse him said how many were the men who knew better not to err than

282. His inhuman cruelty. Note that Machiavelli calls it the "principal cause" of Hannibal's "admirable actions."

283. The argument against the plain sense of the passage — Machiavelli's inclusion of human cruelty among the virtues — is given by Giuseppe Lisio in his *Il Principe di Niccolò Machiavelli* (Florence, 1921), p. 100, n. 15: "By other he means the virtues he had other than cruelty, different from cruelty. . . . I well understand there is a bit of ambiguity; but Machiavelli is not stylistically a perfect writer." Like Lisio, all who contend that Machiavelli does not intend the plain sense of the passage must argue that Machiavelli was a "writer of little consideration."

284. *Conveniva.* Here, convenience means propriety with an undertone of necessity. Scipio gave his army more leniency than was proper. In the previous paragraph, convenience means just what we mean by it: the prince can rightfully kill when the deed offers good chances of favorable results.

to correct errors. That nature, if he had persevered with it in the empire;[285] with time, would have blemished Scipio's fame and glory, but living under the government of the Senate, this harmful quality of his not *solum*[286] was hidden, but was his glory.

I conclude, therefore, returning to being feared and loved, that since men love at their own pleasure and fear at the prince's pleasure, a wise prince must base himself upon that which is his, not upon that which is other men's: he must contrive only to escape hatred, as was said.

285. *nello imperio*, meaning either "into the time of the empire" or in command.
286. Latin for "not only": mock solemnity.

XVIII

Quomodo fides a principibus sit servanda
(In what way faith is to be kept
by princes)

How laudable it is for a prince to keep faith, and to live with integrity and not guile, everyone perceives: nonetheless, in our times one sees by experience that the princes who have done great things are the ones who have taken little account of faith,[287] and who have known to turn men's brains with guile: and in the end have surpassed those who grounded themselves on loyalty.

You[288] therefore must know there are two kinds[289] of fighting: the one with laws, the other with force: the first is proper to man, the second to beasts: but because many times the first does not suffice, it is expedient[290] to recur to the second. Therefore, it is necessary for a prince to know well how to use the beast and the man. This part[291] was taught to princes covertly by the ancient writers, who write that Achilles, and many other ancient princes, were given to Chiron, the centaur, to be nourished that he might raise them under his discipline. To have for preceptor a half-beast and half-man means nothing other than that a prince needs to know how to use both natures; and the one without the other is not durable.

Therefore, since a prince is constrained by necessity to know well how to use the beast, among [the beasts] he must choose the fox and the lion; because the lion does not defend itself from traps, the fox does not defend itself from the wolves. One therefore needs to be a fox to recognize traps, and a lion to dismay the wolves. Those who simply stand on the lion do not

287. della fede means equally "of faith" (i.e., of trustworthiness) and "of the faith" (i.e., of the Christian faith). Machiavelli's reference to Alexander VI below makes clear that he considers being deceitfully un-Christian a requirement for success.

288. Plural.

289. *Generazione*, "generations."

290. *Conviene*, it is convenient, or necessary, or proper, or expedient — indeed, all of the above.

291. *Parte*, also "decision," "choice," "chosen role."

know what they are doing.[292] Therefore, a prudent lord cannot, nor must he, observe faith, when such observance can turn against him[293] and when the causes that made him promise it are extinguished. And if men were all good, this precept would not be good; but because they are sad[294] and they would not observe it with you, you *etiam*[295] do not have to observe it with them. Nor ever did a prince lack legitimate causes with which to color inobservance. One could give infinite modern examples of this and show how much peace, how many promises have been made void and vain by the infidelity of princes: and how the one who has better known to use the fox has come out better. But it is necessary to know well how to color this nature, and to be a great simulator and dissimulator: and men are so simple and so obey present necessities that he who deceives will always find someone who will let himself be deceived.

I do not want to be silent about one of the fresh examples. Alexander VI never did anything, never thought of anything other than to deceive men, and always found subjects to whom he could do it. And never was there a man who had greater success in asserting, and with greater oaths in affirming a thing, who observed it less; nonetheless, the deceptions always succeeded for him *ad votum*,[296] because he knew well this part[297] of the world.

For a prince, therefore, it is not necessary to have all the above-mentioned qualities, but it is judged necessary to appear to have them. Rather,[298] I will

292. *"Non se ne intendono,"* idiomatic, signifying lack of specific expertise. Cf. the use of *intendere* in the first sentence of this chapter, and in the Epistle Dedicatory.

293. *Le torni contro,* "work against him." Cf. Grotius's famous rule *"Pacta sunt servanta rebus sic stantibus,"* which means "Treaties are to be observed, conditions remaining the same." When fulfillment of a commitment ceases to be advantageous, the commitment is *ipso facto* inoperative. This is the modern rule for all human relationships, including marriage.

294. *Tristi,* i.e., a sad, bad lot.

295. Latin, "also," "equally." Machiavelli is investing infidelity with solemnity, and will crown his point with the papal crown.

296. Latin, "according to his desire." This is a charming portrait of a Pope who did *nothing* but deceive people, and succeeded religiously in this, since he was a master of the ways of this world.

297. *Parte* here means both "role" and "aspect." Alexander knew in an exemplary manner the secular side of the world, the side that Machiavelli is describing.

298. *Anzi* means also "even more."

be so daring[299] as to say this, that, having them and observing them always, they are harmful, while appearing to have them is useful; like appearing piteous, faithful, humane, integral, religious, and [perhaps even] to be; but while keeping one's spirit predisposed so that, needing not to be those things, you might know how to change to be the contrary. And let this be perceived,[300] that a prince, and especially a new prince, cannot observe all those things by which men are considered good, it often being necessary to maintain the state, to operate against faith, against charity, against humaneness, against religion. And therefore it is necessary that he have a spirit disposed to turn as the winds and the variations of fortune command him, and, as I said above, not to depart from good when he can, but to know how to enter into evil when he needs to.

Therefore, a prince must have great care that nothing ever leave his mouth that is not full of the above-written five qualities, and that to see him and hear him, he appear all piety, all faith, all integrity, all humaneness, all religion. And there is nothing more necessary to seem to have than this last quality. And men in general judge more by the eyes[301] than by the hands; because to see is for everyone, to feel for a few. Everyone sees what you appear, few feel what you are; and those few who do, dare not oppose themselves to the opinion of many, who have the majesty of the state to defend them: and in the actions of all men and especially of princes, where there is no judgment to call upon, one looks to the results. Therefore, let a prince win and keep the state: and the means will always be judged honorable and lauded by everyone; because the vulgar[302] are taken by what seems and by the outcome of the thing; and in the world there are only the vulgar; and the few don't stand a chance against them when the many have someone upon whom to lean. A certain prince of present times, whom it is better not to name,[303] never preaches anything but peace and faith, and he is most hostile to both one and the other; had he observed both, he would have had either his reputation or his state taken from him many times.

299. *Ardirò* also means, perhaps *very* ironically, "I will burn." People had been burned for utterances far less subversive than the ones in the previous paragraphs.

300. *Et* (Lat.) *lassi ad intendere questo.* The sentence has the sense of "and get this!"

301. By means of the eyes.

302. The populace.

303. Clearly, this is the pope reigning at the time, Julius II.

XIX

De contemptu et odio fugiendo
(On fleeing contempt and hatred)

But because I have spoken concerning the most important of the qualities mentioned above, I want to discuss the others briefly under this category: that, as was said above in part, the prince should think of avoiding those things which might make him hateful and contemptible; and whenever he avoids them, he will have done his part and will not find danger in the other infamies. Above all, as I said, it makes one hateful to be rapacious and usurping of the subjects' things and women: from which he must abstain; and whenever one takes neither things nor honor from the general run of men, they live contented, and one only has to fight against the ambition of the few, which one brakes in many ways, and with ease. It makes one contemptible to be held variable, light, effeminate, pusillanimous, irresolute: which a prince must avoid as he would a shoal, and to scheme[304] so that greatness, spiritedness, gravity, strength might be recognized from his actions, and to insist that his word be irrevocable concerning the private dealings of the subjects; and that he maintain himself in such repute that no one might think either of deceiving him or of getting around him.

The prince who gives this opinion of himself is quite well reputed; and one conspires with difficulty against whomever is reputed; provided it be perceived that he be excellent and revered by his own, he is attacked with difficulty. Because a prince must have two fears: one within, on account of the subjects, the other without, on account of external potentates. Against the latter one defends with good arms and with good friends; and always if he has good arms, he will have good friends; and always when things outside stay firm, they will stay firm inside, if yet they are not perturbed by a conspiracy; and if he has ordained and lived as I said, if he does not abandon himself, he will always bear every shock even if things outside were in motion, as I said Nabis of Sparta did.[305] But, concerning the subjects, when things outside do not move, one has to fear lest they conspire secretly: concerning

304. *Ingegnarsi*, to think up some ingenious scheme whereby.

305. But, of course, since Nabis, who was able to stand up to the Roman armies (Chap. XI), was assassinated by conspirators, this point is to be taken with special caution. *The Prince* is not a book of political recipes.

which, the prince assures himself sufficiently by avoiding being hated or despised, and by keeping the people satisfied with him: which thing it is necessary to achieve, as was said at length above. And one of the most powerful remedies that a prince has against conspiracies is not to be hated by the generality of men, because he who conspires believes to satisfy the people by the death of the prince; but when he believes he would offend it[306] [thereby], he is discouraged from taking such a part, because the difficulties on the conspirators' side are infinite. And, by experience, one sees that conspiracies have been many, and few have had a good end. Because he who conspires cannot be alone, but he can keep company only with those whom he believes to be malcontent; and as soon as you have uncovered your spirit to a malcontent, you give him material with which to make himself content, because manifestly he can hope every comfort from it;[307] so much so that, seeing a firm gain on this side, and seeing the other doubtful and full of danger, he must[308] indeed be either a rare friend, or a wholly obstinate enemy of the prince, to keep faith with you. And, to reduce the thing to brief terms, I say that on the part of the conspirator there is only fear, jealousy, and the thought of penalty which dismays him; but on the part of the prince there is the majesty of the principality, the laws, the defenses of friends and of the state which defend him; so that, when popular benevolence is added to all these things, it is impossible that anyone be so foolishly daring as to conspire. Because, ordinarily, where a conspirator has to fear before the execution of the evil, in this case he also has to fear afterward, once the excess[309] has occurred, not being able to hope for any refuge, since he has the people for an enemy.

One could give infinite examples of this matter. But I only want to be content with one, within the memory of our fathers. Messer Annibale Bentivogli, grandfather of the present Messer Annibale, who was prince of Bologna, having been killed by the Canneschi[310] who conspired against him,

306. I.e., the generality of men.

307. That is, he can expect a big reward for betraying the conspiracy.

308. *Conviene.* The sense is that he *had better be* your very good friend because it will be convenient for him to turn you in. Note that the statement below, "it is impossible that anyone be so foolishly daring . . . ," is absurd on its face and contradicted by the rest of the chapter.

309. I.e., the regicide.

310. Bentivogli was killed by Battista Canneschi in June 1445 in cooperation with Filippo Maria Visconti of Milan. Note that the conspiracy succeeded. Cf. the first sentence of the following paragraph. Anyone who takes it literally deserves whatever trouble he might reap thereby.

nor any of his own surviving other than Messer Giovanni, who was in swaddling clothes, the people rose right away after that homicide and killed all the Canneschi. Which sprang from the popular good will which the Bentivogli house had in those times: which was such that, there not remaining any one of them in Bologna who could govern the state, Annibale being dead, and there being indications that in Florence there was a Bentivogli who until then was the son of a blacksmith, the Bolognesi came for him in Florence, and they gave him the government of that city: which was governed by him until Messer Giovanni could reach the age suitable for government.

I, therefore, conclude that a prince must take little account of conspiracies, when the people are benevolent toward him; but when they are hostile to him and hate him, he must fear everything and everybody. And the well-ordered states and the wise princes have thought with every diligence not to drive the great to despair and to satisfy the people and to keep it contented; because this is one of the most important matters that concern a prince. Among the well-ordered and -governed kingdoms of our times is that of France; and in it are found infinitely good constitutions on which depend the liberty and security of the king, of which the first is the parliament and its authority. Because the one who ordained that kingdom,[311] knowing the ambition of the powerful and their insolence, and judging it necessary that they have a bit in their mouths to correct them, and, on the other hand, knowing the fear-based hate of the general run of men against the great, and wanting to reassure them, he did not want this to be a particular care of the king. Therefore, to take from him the burden that he might have with the great when he favored the people, and with the people when he favored the great, he constituted a third judge, to be the one who would beat down the great and favor the small without burden to the king. This order could not have been better nor more prudent, nor a greater cause of security for the king and the kingdom. From this one may draw another notable thing: that princes need to have burdensome things administered by others, [while they administer] graces by themselves. Again I conclude that a prince must esteem the great but not make himself hated by the people.

It might appear to many, considering the life and death of some Roman emperors, that they might be examples contrary to this opinion of mine,

311. Of course, no one person had "ordained" the kingdom of France. Its ancient institutions had grown slowly and feudally. Moreover, the French parliaments of Machiavelli's time did nothing of the sort that Machiavelli describes. In fact, the French monarchy rested on the king's own army, paid by him with funds that that very army helped extract from the people regardless of parliament.

finding someone who has always lived egregiously and shown great virtue of spirit, who nonetheless lost the empire, or even[312] was killed by his own, who conspired against him. Therefore, because I want to respond to these objections, I will discuss the qualities of some emperors, showing that the causes of their ruin are not incongruent with what has been demonstrated by me; and in part I will offer for consideration those things which are noteworthy to whomever reads the doings of those times. And I want that it suffice for me to take all those emperors who acceded to the empire from Marcus the philosopher to Maximus: who were Marcus, Commodius, his son Pertinax, Julius, Severus, Antonius Caracalla his son, Macrinus, Heliogabalus, Alexander, and Maximus. *Et*[313] it is first to be noted that, where in other principalities one only has to contend with the ambition of the great and the insolence of the peoples, the Roman emperors had a third difficulty, to have to bear the cruelty and avarice of the soldiers. Which thing was so difficult that it caused the ruin of many, it being so difficult to satisfy the soldiers and the peoples; because the peoples loved quiet, and because of this they loved the modest princes, and the soldiers loved the prince who was of military spirit, and who was insolent, cruel, and rapacious. Which qualities they wanted him to practice[314] on the peoples, so as to have double pay and to vent their avarice and cruelty. These[315] always were the ruin of those emperors who, by nature or by art, did not have a great reputation, such as to keep both in check; and most of them, especially those who came to the principality as new men, recognizing the difficulties from these two different humors, turned to satisfy the soldiers, deeming it a small thing to injure the people. Which choice[316] was necessary: because the princes, not being able to avoid being hated by some, must first[317] strain not to be hated

312. Italian *vero*, "truly."

313. Latin, "and."

314. The soldiers wanted the emperors to work insolence, rapacity, and cruelty upon the peoples.

315. These qualities. Notice that Machiavelli has shifted from arguing that polities are composed of three constituencies — the great, the people, and the soldiers — to arguing that there are only two: the peoples and the soldiers. Remember his contention that the prince must favor the people over the great. *Now he argues that the prince must favor the soldiers, soldiers who are his very own, over the people (as well as over the great) — exactly what the king of France was doing.*

316. *Parte.*

317. First only in the order of time, since Machiavelli says immediately after what is first in the order of importance.

by the general public; and when they cannot achieve this, they must devise with every effort to avoid the hatred of the most powerful publics. And therefore the emperors who had need of extraordinary favors because of newness adhered to the soldiers rather than to the peoples: which, nonetheless, turned out to be useful or not to them according to whether that prince knew how to keep himself reputed by them. It sprang from these abovementioned causes that Marcus, Pertinax, and Alexander, being modest in life, lovers of justice, enemies of cruelty, humane and benign, all had a sad end, except for Marcus. Only Marcus lived and died most honored, because he had succeeded to the empire *iure hereditario*,[318] and did not have to be grateful for it either to the soldiers or to the peoples; moreover, being accompanied by many virtues which made him venerable, he always kept both the other orders within bounds [set by himself] while he lived, and was never hated nor despised. But Pertinax was made emperor against the will of the soldiers who, being accustomed to live licentiously under Commodius, could not bear the honest life to which Pertinax wanted to reduce them; because of this, having created hatred for himself and added disdain to this hatred because he was old, he came to ruin at the very beginning of his administration.

And here one must note that hatred is acquired through good works as well as by nasty ones; and therefore, as I said above, a prince who wants to keep the state is often forced to be not good; because when the constituency which you need to maintain yourself is corrupt, be they people or soldiers or great ones, it is convenient for you[319] to follow its humor to satisfy it, and then good works are your enemies. But let us come to Alexander: who was of such goodness that among the other lauds which are attributed to him is this, that in the fourteen years that he held the empire, no one was ever killed by him unjudged: nonetheless, Alexander being considered effeminate and a man who let himself be ruled by his mother, and having come into contempt for this, the army conspired against him and killed him.

Discussing now, by contrast, the qualities of Commodius, of Severus, Antonius, Caracalla, and Maximus, you[320] will find them most cruel and most rapacious: who, to satisfy the soldiers, did not exclude[321] any kind of injury which might be committed against the people; and all, except Sev-

318. Latin, "by right of inheritance."

319. Italian *ti conviene*, singular, very familiar.

320. Plural.

321. Italian *perdonarono*, literally, "pardon," but obviously meaning "exclude."

erus, had a sad end. Because there was so much virtue in Severus that because he kept the soldiers friendly, he was always able to reign happily, though the people might be weighed down by him; because those virtues of his made him so admirable in the sight of the soldiers and of the peoples that the latter remained *quodammodo*[322] stunned and stupefied, and the former reverent and satisfied. And because the actions of this man were great in a new prince, I want to show briefly how well he knew to use the persons of the fox and the lion: which natures I say above are necessary for a prince to imitate. Severus, having recognized the indolence of the emperor Julian, persuaded his army, of which he was captain in Slavonia, that it was good for him to go to Rome to avenge the death of Pertinax, who had been killed by the praetorian soldiers; and under this color, without showing that he aspired to the empire, he moved his army against Rome; and he was in Italy before anyone knew of his departure. Once arrived in Rome, he was elected emperor by the Senate out of fear and he killed Julian. After this beginning, two difficulties remained to Severus's desire to make himself lord of all the state: the one in Asia, where Nigrus, chief of the Asian armies, had himself called emperor, and the other in the west, where there was Albinus, who also aspired to the empire. And because he judged it dangerous to uncover himself as the enemy of both, he determined to attack Nigrus and to deceive Albinus. To whom he wrote that, having been elected emperor by the Senate, he wanted to share that dignity with him; and he sent him the title of Caesar, and joined to himself as colleague by deliberation of the Senate: which things were accepted as true by Albinus. But once Severus had defeated and killed Nigrus and pacified things in the Orient, having returned to Rome, he complained[323] in the Senate that Albinus, hardly grateful for the benefits received from him, had perfidiously tried to kill him, and for this reason it was necessary that he go punish his ingratitude. Thereafter, he went to meet him in France and took from him the state and his life.

Therefore, whoever examines minutely the actions of this man will find him a most ferocious lion and a most astute fox, and will see him feared and revered by everyone, and not hated by the armies, and will not marvel that he, a new man, would have held so much empire: because his very great reputation always defended him from that hatred that the peoples could have conceived because of his depredations. But Antonius, his son, was a

322. Latin, "in a certain way." Note that Severus, like Cesare Borgia, was able to render his subjects "satisfied" and "stupefied." Like Borgia, Machiavelli offers him as an example to be imitated.

323. *Si querelò*, reflexive, "quarreled himself with."

man who had excellent parts[324] and which made him marvelous in the sight of the peoples, and welcome to the soldiers; because he was a military man and most adept at bearing any toil, despiser of every delicate food and of every other softness: which made him loved by all the armies. Nonetheless, his ferocity and cruelty were so great and so unheard of because, after infinite individual killings, he had killed a great part of the people of Rome, and all of Alexandria, so that he became most hateful to all the world; and he began to be feared *etiam*[325] by those he had around him: such that he was killed by a centurion, the midst of his army. Here it is to be noted that deaths such as this, which follow by the deliberation of an obstinate spirit, are unavoidable by princes, because anyone who does not care about dying can strike him; but the prince must fear them less, because they are most rare. He must only guard against doing grave injury to one of those whom he uses and whom he has around him in the service of his principality: as Antonius had done, who had killed in an outrageous manner a brother of that centurion and threatened him every day; *tamen*[326] he kept him as a bodyguard: which was a daring and ruinous part,[327] as it turned out to be.

But let us come to Commodius, who kept the empire with great ease because he had it *jure hereditario*,[328] being son of Marcus; and it would have sufficed him to follow in his father's tracks[329] and he would have satisfied the soldiers and the peoples, but, being of cruel and bestial spirit, in order to work his rapacity on the peoples, he turned to indulging[330] the armies and to making them licentious; on the other hand, not reserving his dignity, often descending into the theaters to fight with gladiators, and doing other things most vile and little worthy of the imperial majesty, he became contemptible in the sight of the soldiers. And being hated on one side and despised on the other, he was conspired against, and killed.

It remains to us to narrate the qualities of Maximus. This was a most bellicose man; and the armies being bothered by Alexander's softness, which I discussed above, having killed him, they elected him to the empire. Which he did not possess very long; because two things made him hateful

324. *Parte*, here "qualities."
325. Latin, "even."
326. Latin, "even so," "nevertheless."
327. *Partito*, "choice."
328. Latin, "by right of inheritance."
329. *Vestigie*, "vestiges."
330. *Intrattenere*, literally, "entertain," "favor."

and contemptible: one is that he was most vile, having previously guarded[331] sheep in Thrace (which thing was most well known and caused great disdain for him in everyone's regard); the other was that because, having put off going to Rome and entering into the possession of the imperial seat at the beginning of his principality, he had given the impression of himself as most cruel, since he had committed many cruelties through his prefects, in Rome and everywhere else in the empire. So that, the whole world being moved by disdain for the vileness of his blood and by hate for fear of his ferocity, first Africa rebelled, followed by the Senate with all the people of Rome; and all Italy conspired against him. His own army joined them; which [army, while] besieging Aquileia and finding difficulty in taking it, bothered by his cruelty, and fearing him less because it saw so many enemies, killed him.

I do not wish to reason either of Heliogabalus, or of Macrinus, or of Julian, who, because they were entirely contemptible, were extinguished right away; but I will come to the conclusion of this discourse. And I say that as the princes of our time govern, they have less difficulty satisfying the soldiers extraordinarily well; because notwithstanding that one has to have some consideration for them, *tamen*,[332] it is quickly resolved, for none of these princes have armies that are integrated with the government and administration of the provinces, as were the armies of the Roman empire. And so, if at that time it was necessary to satisfy the soldiers more than the peoples, it was because soldiers could do more than the peoples; now it is necessary to all princes, except for the Turk and the sultan, to satisfy the people rather than the soldiers, because the former people can do[333] more than the latter. From this I except the Turk, since he always keeps around him twelve thousand infantrymen and fifteen thousand horses, on which the security and the strength of his kingdom depend; and it is necessary for that lord that he keep them as friends before any other consideration.[334] Similarly, since the kingdom of the sultan is all in the hands of soldiers, it is convenient that he too keep them friends without regard[335] to the peoples. And you[336] have to note that this state of the sultan is incongruent with all other principalities; because it is similar to the Christian papacy, which one

331. *Guardato*, "looked at" and "guarded." He had been a lowly shepherd.
332. Latin, "nevertheless."
333. *Possono*, i.e., can wield more power.
334. *Rispetto*, "respect."
335. *Rispetto*, "respect."
336. Plural.

cannot call either a hereditary principality nor a new principality; because it is not the children of the old prince who inherit and remain lords, but he who is elected to that rank by those who have the authority. And since this order is ancient,[337] one cannot call it a new principality, because in it are none of the difficulties that are in the new ones; because even though the prince is new, the orders of that state are old, and they are ordered to receive him as if he were their hereditary lord.

But let us return to our subject. I say whoever will consider the above-mentioned discourse will see that either hate or contempt was the cause of the ruin of those above-mentioned emperors and will also recognize the reason why some of them had a happy end and the others an unhappy one, even though part of them proceeded in one mode and part in the contrary. Because it was futile and dangerous for Pertinax and Alexander, being new princes, to want to imitate Marcus, who was in the principality *jure heredi-tario*;[338] and similarly for Caracalla, Commodius, and Maximus, it was a pernicious thing to have imitated Severus, since they did not have enough virtue to allow them to follow his tracks. Therefore, a new prince in a new principality cannot imitate the actions of Marcus, nor yet is it necessary to follow those of Severus; but he must take from Severus those parts which are necessary to found his state and from Marcus those which are convenient and glorious to conserve a state that is already established and firm.

---

337. *Antiquato*, also "antiquated."
338. Latin, "by right of inheritance."

XX

An arces et multa alia quae cotidie a principibus fiunt utilia an inutilia sint (Whether fortresses and many other things which everyday are done by princes are useful or useless)

To hold the state securely, some princes have disarmed their subjects; others have kept subject lands divided; some have nourished enmities against themselves; others have tried to gain those who were suspect to them at the beginning of their state; some have built fortresses; some have ruined and destroyed them. And even though one may not be able to give definitive judgments on all these things, without dealing with the particulars of states in which one must take some similar decision, nonetheless, I will speak broadly, as the subject itself requires.

Thus, there never was any reason why[339] a new prince should disarm his subjects; on the contrary, when he finds them disarmed, he should always arm them; because by arming them, those arms become yours, those whom you suspected become faithful, and those who were faithful keep themselves so, and the subjects make themselves partisans. And because one cannot arm all subjects, if you benefit those whom you arm, you can do [what you like] to the others more securely: and that difference in treatment which they recognize in their own regard makes them obliged to you, while the others excuse you, judging it necessary for these to have more merit because they have more danger and more obligation. But when you disarm them, you begin to offend them, you show you distrust them either out of vileness or out of little faith: and both these opinions generate[340] hate against you. And because you cannot stay unarmed, it is convenient that you turn to the mercenary militia, which is of the above-mentioned quality; and when it is good, it cannot be so good as to defend you against powerful enemies and suspect subjects. But, as I have said, a new prince of a new

339. Italian *che*, literally, "that."
340. *Concepe*, conceive.

principality always has ordained arms in it. The histories are full of such examples. But when a prince acquires a new state that is added to his own as a member, then it is necessary to disarm that state, except for those who have been your partisans in acquiring it; and with time and with occasions, it is necessary to render them also soft and effeminate, and to order oneself so that all the arms of your state be in soldiers of your own, who live in your old state close to you.

Our ancient ones,[341] and those who were esteemed wise, used to say that it was necessary to keep Pistoia with parties[342] and Pisa with fortresses; and by this they nourished differences in some lands subject to them to possess them more easily. This had to be done indeed in the days when Italy was balanced in a certain way,[343] but I do not believe that divisions ever did any good; on the contrary, when the enemy approaches, divided cities are necessarily lost right away; because the weakest part will always adhere to the outside forces and the others will not be able to bear up.

The Venetians, moved, as I believe, by the above-written reasons, fostered the Guelph and Ghibelline sects in the cities subject to them; and even though they never let them come to blood, *tamen*[344] they nourished these contrary opinions, so that citizens occupied by those differences of theirs could not unite against them. Which, as one saw, did not thereafter turn out as they intended; because after they were broken at Vaila,[345] one of those parties right away got daring, and took from them all the state. Therefore, such modes betoken[346] weakness in the prince, because in a confident[347] principality such divisions will never be permitted; because they profit him only in time of peace, by making the subjects more easily manageable; but when war comes, such orders show their flaw.

Without doubt, princes become great when they overcome the difficulties and the opposition raised against them; and therefore fortune, especially when she wishes to make great a new prince, who has greater need to

341. I.e., our forefathers. Here Machiavelli is not referring to the true ancients, the Romans, whom he deemed truly wise, but to "our" ancients, the ones who were purported to be wise by the Florentines of his time.

342. I.e., by counterposing factions to one another.

343. I.e., before Charles VIII descended into Italy in 1494.

344. Latin, "nevertheless."

345. The cities of Brescia, Verona, Vicenza, and Padua rebelled against Venetian rule after Venice's defeat at Vaila in May 1509.

346. *Arguiscono*, "argue for."

347. *Galiardo*, here used in the literal sense of cocky, self-assured.

acquire reputation than a hereditary one, it makes enemies spring up for him, and it makes him do campaigns against them so that he might have occasion to overcome them, and climb up high by the ladder that his enemies have brought him. Therefore, many judge that a wise prince must nourish some enmity when he has the occasion, so that, having suppressed it, more greatness for him might follow.

Princes and *praesertim*[348] those who are new, have found more faith and more usefulness in men who were suspect in the beginning of their state than in those whom they trusted in the beginning. Pandolfo Petrucci, prince of Siena, governed the state more with those who had been suspect to him than with the others. But one cannot speak broadly of this thing, because it varies according to individuals. I will only say this, that the prince will always be able to gain with very great ease those men who in the beginning of a principality had been enemies, who are the kind who need to lean upon others to bear themselves up: and they are more powerfully forced to serve him with faith, insomuch as they know it is more necessary for them to erase with works that sinister opinion which one had of them. And thus the prince always draws greater utility from them than from those who, serving with too much security, neglect his things.

And, because the subject calls for it, I do not want to leave out recalling to princes who have newly taken a state through favors within it[349] that they consider well what purpose[350] might have moved those who favored him to favor him; and if it is not natural affection toward them, but if it were only because those [who favored the new prince] were not content with [the former] state, he will be able to keep them his friends with toil and great difficulties, because it is impossible that he succeed in contenting them. And, discussing the cause of this well with examples taken from things ancient and modern, he will see that it is much easier for him to gain for himself as friends those men who were content with the previous state, and therefore were his enemies, than those who, because they were not content with it, became friends with him and helped him occupy it.

It has been the custom of princes, in order more securely to hold their

---

348. Latin, "especially." It is difficult to escape the feeling that when Machiavelli sprinkles his discussion with Latin, his tongue is deeply in his cheek. This is especially the case here, where he is sending yet another of his commercial messages to Lorenzo: You ought to consider employing me even though I belonged to the party that you defeated when you took power.

349. *Intrinsici di quello*, "intrinsic to it."

350. *Cagione*, "cause."

state, to build fortresses, that they might be bridle and a bit for those who might scheme against them, and to have a secure refuge from sudden attack. I laud this mode, because it has been used since ancient times:[351] nonetheless, in our times, Messer Niccolo Vitelli, himself has seen two fortresses undone in the city of Castello to keep that state.[352] Guido Ubaldo, duke of Urbino, having returned to his dominion, whence he had been chased by Cesare Borgia, ruined all the fortresses of that province *funditis*;[353] and judged that without them he would lose that state again with greater difficulty. When Bentivogli returned to Bologna, he used similar measures. Therefore, fortresses are useful or not according to the times; and, if they do you good in one part,[354] they hurt you in another. And this part can be discussed thus. That prince who is more afraid of the peoples than of foreigners, must make fortresses; but the one who is more afraid of foreigners than of the people, must leave them out. The castle of Milan, which Francesco Sforza built there, has made and will make more war against the Sforza house than any other disorder of that state. But the best fortress that can exist is not to be hated by the people; because if the people hate you, even if you have fortresses they do not save you; because, once they have taken arms, peoples will never lack foreigners to help[355] them. In our times, one does not see that they have profited any prince, if not the countess of Forlì, when Count Girolamo, her consort, was killed; because by means of it she was able to flee the people's attack and wait for help from Milan, and take back the state. And the circumstances then were such that the foreigner could not help the people; but later, when Cesare Borgia attacked, the fortresses were worth little to her, and her hostile people joined with the foreigner. Therefore, then and before, it would have been more secure for her not to be hated by the people than to have had fortresses. Therefore, all these things considered, I will laud whoever makes fortresses and whoever does not, and I will blame whoever, trusting in fortresses, thinks little of being hated by the people.

351. Italian *d'antiquo.*

352. In 1482, Vitelli retook Città da Castello from the pope, and subsequently destroyed the two fortresses which the latter had built there. Security lies in political arrangements, not in masonry work.

353. Latin, "to the foundations."

354. Italian *parte*, "place" or "situation."

355. Subjunctive.

XXI

Quod principem deceat ut egregius habeatur
(What is convenient to a prince
that he might be esteemed)

Nothing makes a prince so esteemed as doing great enterprises and giving rare examples of himself. In our times we have Ferdinand of Aragon, present king of Spain. This one can be called almost a new prince, because from a weak king he has become the first king of the Christians in fame and glory; and if you will consider his actions, you[356] will find them all very great and some extraordinary. In the beginning of his reign he attacked Granada,[357] and that enterprise was the foundation of his state. First, he did it at ease,[358] and without fear of being opposed: in it he kept occupied the spirits of the barons of Castille, who, thinking of the war, did not think of innovating, and by that means he acquired reputation and power[359] over them, which they were not aware of. With the money of the Church and of the peoples, he was able to nourish armies and with that long war made a foundation for his militia, which thereafter honored him. Beyond this, in order to undertake greater enterprises, always availing himself of[360] religion, he turned to a pious cruelty, despoiling the Marranos and chasing them from his reign,[361] nor can this example be more miserable nor more rare. Under the same cloak he attacked Africa; did the Italian enterprise;[362] lately he has attacked France, and thus always he has done and schemed

356. Plural.

357. The birth of modern Spain dates from the war against Moorish Granada (1480–1492).

358. I.e., when he and his kingdom were otherwise at rest. "It" in this and the following sentence refers to the war.

359. *Imperio*, "empire."

360. *Servendosi*, literally, serving himself with, i.e., using religion as a pretext and tool, as his servant. Machiavelli could have used a less affective word. But he chose to leave no doubt.

361. Marranos means pigs. Ferdinand rid himself of those who would not eat pig, that is, of the Muslims and Jews. These were the subjects of his "pious cruelty."

362. The taking of the Kingdom of Naples in 1500.

great things, which have always held the spirits of his subjects in suspense and admiration; and preoccupied with their success. And these actions of his sprang one from another, which has never given time between one and another for men to be able to work calmly against him.

It also benefits a prince considerably to give rare examples of himself in internal governance, similar to those which are told of Messer Bernabò of Milan,[363] whenever the topic[364] arises of someone who accomplishes extraordinary things in civil life; either good or evil, and of choosing ways of rewarding or punishing; of which much will be said. And above all a prince must scheme to give himself the fame of a great man and of excellent judgment[365] in every action. A prince is also esteemed when he is a true friend and a true enemy, that is to say, when he comes out in favor of one against another without hesitation.[366] Which part[367] will always be more useful than to remain neutral; because if two powerful neighbors of yours come to blows,[368] either they are such that, one of them winning, you have to fear the winner, or not. In whichever of these two cases, it will always be more useful to you to come out openly and make a good war; because in the first case, if you do not come out, you will always be the prey of whoever wins, with the pleasure and satisfaction of the vanquished, and you have neither reason nor anything that might defend you or that might give you shelter. Because he who wins does not want suspect friends who did not help him in adversity; he who loses does not shelter you, because you did not want to rescue his fortune with arms in hand.

Antiochus had passed into Greece, having been put there by the Aetolians to chase the Romans out of it. Antiochus sent ambassadors to the Acheans, who were friends of the Romans, to urge them[369] to stay in the middle, while from the other side the Romans were persuading them to take up arms for them. This matter came to be deliberated in the council of the Acheans, where Antioch's legate was persuading them to remain neutral, to which the Roman legate answered: "Concerning what these tell you, that it

363. Barnabò Visconti gained power in Milan in 1355 by murdering his brother. He held it until 1385 by legendary cruelty, and died poisoned.

364. *Occasione*, literally, "occasion."

365. *Ingegno*, "thought" or "genius."

366. Italian *rispetto*, literally, respect.

367. I.e., choice.

368. Literally, "to hands."

369. Literally, "to comfort them."

is more convenient for you not to intervene in the war, nothing is farther from your interest; without favors, without dignity, you will be the trophy of the victor."[370] And it will always happen that he who is not a friend will seek your neutrality, and he who is your friend will ask you to come out with arms. And ill-resolute[371] princes most often follow that neutral way in order to avoid present perils, and most often ruin. But when the prince comes out gallantly in favor of one side, if the one to whom you adhere wins, although he is powerful and you remain at his discretion, he has an obligation to you and love has been contracted; and men are never so dishonest that they oppress you with such an example of ingratitude. Moreover, victories are never so neat that the victor does not have to have some respect,[372] and especially for justice. But if the one to whom you adhere loses, you are sheltered by him; and he helps you while he can, and you become the comrade of a fortune that can rise again. In the second case, when those who fight against one another are such that you do not have to fear the one who wins, the prudence of taking sides is so much the greater; because you assist in the ruin of one with the help of the other who should save him, if he were wise; and when he has won, he remains at your discretion; and, with your help, it is impossible that he not win.

And here it is to be noted that a prince must take care never to join with one more powerful than himself to harm others, unless need grips him, as was said above; because, winning, you remain his prisoner: and princes must avoid being at others' discretion as much as they can. The Venetians teamed up[373] with France against the duke of Milan, and they could have avoided making that team; from which their ruin resulted. But, when one cannot avoid doing it, as happened to the Florentines, when the pope and Spain went to attack Lombardy with their armies, then the prince must join for the above-mentioned reasons. Nor let him ever believe that a state can always make safe choices; on the contrary, let him think that he must make only doubtful ones; because this is in the order of things, that one never tries to avoid one inconvenience without incurring another; but prudence consists of knowing how to recognize the kinds of inconveniences, and to take the least sad for good.

370. Livy XXV, 49. Inexact quote.

371. Machiavelli could more easily have said "irresolute." But he chose to say *mal resoluti*, badly resolved.

372. I.e., concern.

373. Italian *si accompagnarono*, literally, "accompanied themselves."

A prince must also show himself lover of the virtues, and honor those excellent in art. Accordingly, he must influence[374] his citizens calmly to exercise their functions, in commerce and in agriculture, and in every other function of men, that no one should fear to adorn his possessions for fear that they might be taken from him, and that no one should fear to open a business for fear of taxes; but he must prepare prizes for whoever wants to do these things, and for whoever might think to enlarge his city or his state in whatever way. Beyond this, he must keep the peoples occupied with feasts and spectacles at convenient times of the year. And, because every city is divided into arts or into tribes, he must take into account these categories, meeting with them from time to time, himself giving examples of humaneness and of munificence, nonetheless always keeping firm the majesty of his dignity, because this should never be lacking in anything.

374. Italian *animare*, "animate" or "give spirit to."

XXII

De his quos a secretis principes habent
(Of the secretaries which princes
have by them)

The choice of ministers is of no little importance to a prince: they are good or not according to the prudence of the prince. And the first estimate one makes of a lord's brain is from the sight of the men he has around him; and when they are capable and faithful, one can always deem him wise, because he has known how to recognize them as able and to keep them faithful. But when they are otherwise, one can always make an unfavorable judgment of him; because the first mistake he makes, he makes it in this choice.

There was no one who knew Messer Antonio da Vanafro as minister of Pandolfo Petrucci, prince of Siena, who did not judge Pandolfo to be a most worthy man, because he had him for his minister. And because brains are of three kinds — one that perceives by itself, another that discerns what others perceive, a third that does not perceive either [for] itself or [through] others, that first being most excellent, the second excellent, the third useless — therefore, it was necessarily convenient[375] that, if Pandolfo was not in the first rank, he should have been in the second: because whenever one has the faculty to recognize the good or the evil that another does and says, though he himself does not have inventiveness, he recognizes the sad and the good works of the minister and he exalts the latter and the others he corrects; and the minister cannot hope to deceive him, and keeps himself good.

But as to how a prince may recognize the minister, there is a mode which never fails. When you see the minister think more of himself than of you, and that he seeks what is useful to him in all actions, someone made that way will never be a good minister, never will you be able to trust him: because whoever has another's state in his hand must never think of himself but always of the prince, and never remember anything that does not pertain to him. And from the other side, the prince, in order to keep him good, must think of the minister, honoring him, making him rich, obliging him to himself, sharing with him honors and burdens, so that he might see that he

---

375. *Conveniva . . . di necessità.* Note the redundancy, and the circumlocution that follows. Again, Machiavelli's tongue is deeply in cheek.

cannot stand without him, and that the many honors might not make him want more honors, the many riches not make him want more riches, the many burdens make him fear responsibilities. Therefore, when the ministers and the princes in relation to ministers are made in such ways, they may confide in one another; and when otherwise, the end is always harmful either for the one or for the other.

XXIII

Quomodo adulatores sint fugiendi
(How flatterers are to be fled)

I do not want to leave out one important heading[376] and one error against which princes defend themselves with difficulty if they are not most prudent or if they do not have good judgment. And these are flatterers, of which the courts are full; because men delight so much in their own things, and through them so deceive themselves, that with difficulty they defend themselves against this plague, and in trying to defend against it, one runs the risk of becoming contemptible. Because there is no other way to guard oneself against flattery, if not to get men to perceive that they do not offend you by telling you the truth; but when anyone can tell you the truth, you lack the reverence [of others]. Therefore, a prudent prince must have a third mode, choosing wise men in his state, and only to those must he give license to speak the truth to him, and of those things alone that he asks about and of nothing else; but he must ask them about everything, and hear their opinions; thereafter to deliberate alone, in his own way; and with these councils and with each member of them he must comport himself so that each recognizes that the more freely he speaks, the more it shall be acceptable to him: aside from these he should not want to hear anyone, [should] move directly to the matter that he had decided, and persevere in his decisions. He who does otherwise either falls through flatterers or changes often because of the different opinions [he hears]: from which springs a low estimation of him.

In this regard, I want to bring a modern example. Father Luca,[377] man of the present emperor Maximilian, speaking of his majesty, said that he took counsel with no one, and never did anything in this way: which sprang from adherence to rules contrary to the above-mentioned. Because the emperor is a secret man, he does not communicate his designs to anyone, he does not take their counsel: but as they are being put into effect one begins to know and discover them, they begin to be contradicted by those he has around him; and, since he is easy, he distances himself from them.[378] This is why

---

376. *Capo*, head or chief. He does not want to neglect an important *subject*.

377. *Pre luca. Pre* is a contraction of *prete*, priest.

378. *se ne stoglie*, literally, "he divests himself," that is, he sheds his own policies as people shed clothes.

the things he does one day, he destroys the next; and that one never knows what he wants to or designs to do, and that one cannot ground oneself upon his decisions.

Therefore, a prince must always take counsel, but when he wants, and not when others want; on the contrary, he should discourage[379] everyone from counseling him on anything, if he does not ask it of them; but he indeed must be a broad questioner, and, a patient listener of the truth concerning the things asked; even more so,[380] perceiving that someone is not telling it to him because of some fear,[381] he should become angry. And because many deem that a prince who gives the impression of being prudent is so considered not because of his nature, but because of the good counsel which he has around him, doubtless they are deceived.[382] Because this is a general rule that never fails: that a prince who is not wise himself cannot be well counseled, unless by chance he were to place[383] himself in the hands of one person alone who was a very prudent man, [who would] rule him in everything. In this case, he could well be [well counseled] but would last little, because that ruler in a brief time would take the state from him; but, taking counsel with more than one, a prince who is not wise will never have coherent counsels, nor will he know for himself how to unite them; each of the counselors will think of his own interest;[384] he will not know how to correct them, nor to recognize [them for what they are]. And they cannot be found otherwise; because men will always turn out sad for you, if they are not made good by necessity. Therefore, one concludes that the good counsel, regardless of where it comes from,[385] necessarily springs from the prudence of the prince, and not the prudence of the prince from the good counsel.

379. *torre animo*, literally, "take away spirit."

380. *anzi*, also, on the contrary.

381. *rispetto*, respect.

382. The confusion of singular and plural in this sentence, as in many others, is in the original and causes the attentive reader to strain for meaning. Not surprisingly, the following sentence is especially noteworthy, in that it contradicts all of Chap. XXII, and especially the point made after fn. 1. Indeed, the remainder of the paragraph, elliptically written, reverses the plain sense of the early part of the chapter.

383. I.e., to remit himself wholly.

384. *La proprietà sua*, meaning not "property" so much as "the things which are peculiarly his own."

385. *Da qualunque venghino*, either "from whomever" or "from whatever" quarter.

XXIV

Cur Italiae principes regnum amiserunt (Why the princes of Italy lost their states)

Prudently observed, the above-written things make a new prince seem ancient, and right away they make him more secure and more firm in the state than if he had grown old in it. Because a new prince is observed much more in his actions than a hereditary one; and, when virtues are recognized in him, they grab[386] men more and oblige them much more than do ancient bloodlines. Because men are taken by present things much more than by past ones, and when they find good in the present ones, they enjoy it and do not look elsewhere; even more,[387] when he does not fail to do the rest for himself, they will take every measure on his behalf. And thus he will have double glory, because of having begun a new principality, and adorned it and strengthened it with good laws, with good arms, with good friends, and with good examples; [even] as he who, born a prince, lost it through lack of prudence has double shame.

And if one will consider the lords who have lost their state in Italy in our times, like the king of Naples, the duke of Milan,[388] and others, one will find in them, first, a common defect regarding arms, for the reasons which were discussed at length above; moreover, one will see some of them who either have had hostile peoples or, if he had friendly people, did not know how to make sure of the great: because without these defects, one does not lose states that possess nerve[389] sufficient to keep an army in the field. Philip of Macedon — not the father of Alexander, but the one who was vanquished by Titus Quintus — did not have much state, compared to the greatness of the Romans and of Greece who attacked him; nonetheless, being a military man who knew how to favor the people and make sure of the great, he kept

386. *Pigliano*, they seize or impress.

387. *Anzi*, on the contrary, even more so.

388. Frederick of Aragon, king of Naples, fell in 1500 under the combined attacks of France and Spain. Ludovico il Moro was defeated by Louis XII.

389. I.e., so much sinew.

up the war against them for many years: and if at the end he lost dominion over some cities, the kingdom nonetheless remained to him.

Therefore, these princes of ours, who had been in their principality many years, let them not accuse fortune of having lost them, but rather their own indolence: because, never having thought in calm times that times might change (which is the common defect of men, discounting the storm during the calm), then when adverse times came, they thought to flee rather than to defend themselves; and they hoped that the peoples, bothered by the insolence of the victors, might call them back. This part[390] is good when others are lacking; but it is indeed bad[391] to have left the other remedies for the sake of that one: because no one should ever choose to fall, believing that others might pick [him] up, which either does not happen or, if it happens, it is not your security, because that strategem was vile and not dependent on you. And the only defenses that are good, are certain, are durable, [are the ones] that depend on you yourself and on your virtue.

390. I.e., this chosen path or plan.
391. Literally, "good 'n' bad."

XXV

Quantum fortuna in rebus humanis possit, et quomodo illi sit occurrendum
(How powerful fortune in human things can be, and how it can be resisted)

It is not unknown to me that many have had and have the opinion that the world's things are so governed by fortune and by God that men cannot correct them by their prudence, indeed that they have no remedy at all for it; and because of this they might judge that there was not much [point in] sweating over things, but [that it was rather better] to let oneself be governed by fate. This opinion has been believed more in our times because great changes in things beyond every human conjecture have been seen and are seen every day. Sometimes when I have thought of this I have been in part inclined to their opinion. Nonetheless, so that our free will not be extinguished, I judge it possible that it be true that fortune is the arbiter of half our actions, but also that *etiam*[392] she leaves the other half, or nearly, to be governed by us. And I liken her to one of those ruinous rivers which, when they get angry, flood the plains, ruin the trees and the buildings, take earth from this part and put it elsewhere: everyone flees before them, all yield to the impetus, without being able to bar it anywhere. And even though they are made thus, it does not follow that, when times are calm, men are unable to make provisions, with both dikes and levees, so that, when they rise, either they flow through a canal or their impetus is neither so unruly nor so harmful. It happens similarly with fortune: which shows its power when no virtue is ordained to resist it, and therefore turns its forces whereunto it knows that levees and dikes do not exist to restrain her. And if you consider Italy, which is the seat of the changes and the one which has given them motion, you[393] will see it to be a countryside without levees and without any dike: because if it were protected[394] by convenient[395] virtue, like Germany,

392. Latin, "even so."
393. Plural.
394. *Reparata* (past participle); cf. the noun Machiavelli uses for dike, *riparo*.
395. *Conveniente*, i.e., the virtue necessary to the particular situation.

Spain, and France, either this floodcrest[396] would not have made the great changes which it has, or it would not have come here. And I want this saying to be sufficient as regards opposing oneself to fortune in general.

But, restricting myself to the particulars, I say that today one sees this prince prosper and tomorrow ruin, without having seen them change nature or any quality: I believe that this arises, first, from the causes that were discussed at length above, that is to say, that the prince who leans wholly on fortune comes to ruin as [fortune] varies. I believe, moreover, that whoever adapts his mode of proceeding to the quality of the times is happy; and similarly, he whose procedure disagrees with the times is unhappy. For men proceed noticeably differently in [doing] the things which lead them to the objective that all have before them, namely, glory and riches: one with caution, the other with impetus; one by violence, the other with art; one by patience, the other with its opposite: and each can get there through these different modes. One also sees two cautious persons, one achieving his design, the other not; and similarly, two succeed equally with two different plans, the one cautiously and the other impetuously, this springs from nothing other than the quality of the times to which their procedure conforms or not. From this springs what I said, that two, operating differently, may produce the same effect; and that of two persons operating equally, one gets himself to his goal and the other not. On this also depends the variation of the good[397]: for, if one rules himself with cautions[398] and patience, and the times and conditions turn so that his rule is good, he may come out successful; but if the times and conditions change, he comes to ruin,[399] because he does not change his way of proceeding. Neither is anyone to be found so prudent as to know how to accommodate himself to this; whether because he cannot deviate from that to which nature inclines him, and *etiam*[400] because, having always prospered by walking one path, he cannot persuade himself to depart from it. And therefore, when it is time for the cautious man to come to force, he does not know how to do it; because of which he comes to ruin: because, if he changed nature with the times and with conditions, his fortune would not change.

396. *Piena*, literally, full, but meaning the flood crest of a full river.

397. *La variazione del bene*, literally, the variation of the good. In this murky passage, *bene* certainly means "circumstances." But Machiavelli chose to use the word *good* instead to signify the variation of providence, and above all the central proposition of the book (chap. XV), namely, that what is good is what is useful in any given circumstance.

398. *Rispetti*, respects.

399. *Rovina*, that is, comes to ruin, ruins himself.

400. Latin, equally.

Pope Julius II proceeded impetuously in every affair of his, and he found the times and conditions so congruent to his way of proceeding that a happy end always resulted. Consider[401] the first enterprise[402] that he did in Bologna, while Messer Giovanni Bentivogli still lived. The Venetians were not content with it; the king of Spain the same; he discussed that enterprise with France; and nonetheless, he personally moved that expedition with his ferocity and impetus. This move held Spain and the Venetians still and in suspense, the latter out of fear, and the other out of the desire he had to retake all the kingdom of Naples; and from the other side he dragged the king of France along behind him; because that king having seen him move, and desiring to make a friend of him in order to lower the Venetians, he judged he could not deny him his people without manifestly offending him. Therefore, Julius accomplished with his impetuous move what no other pontiff would have accomplished with all human prudence; because if he had waited to leave Rome until deals[403] were firm and all things in order, as any other pontiff would have done, [the whole thing] would never have come out for him; because the king of France would have had a thousand excuses, and the others raised a thousand fears in him. I want to leave his other actions be, which were all similar, and all turned out well for him; and the brevity of his life did not let him feel the opposite; because, if times had come when it would have been necessary to proceed with caution,[404] his ruin would have resulted from them: for never would he have deviated from the ways to which nature inclined him.

I, therefore, conclude that since fortune varies, and men remain in their obstinate ways, they are happy while they agree with one another, and when they disagree, unhappy. Indeed, I judge this, that it is better to be impetuous than cautious,[405] because fortune is a woman; and if one wants to keep her under, it is necessary to beat her and knock her. And one sees that she lets herself be won more by these than by those who proceed coldly. And so always, like a woman, she is the friend of the young, because they are less cautious,[406] more ferocious, and command her more audaciously.

401. Second person plural.

402. *Impresa* can also mean *presa*, "taking."

403. *Conclusione*, conclusions.

404. *Rispetti*, respects.

405. *Respettivo*, respectful.

406. *Respettivi*, respectful. The point of the passage is: less respect, more audacity win both women and kingdoms.

XXVI

Exhortatio ad capessendam Italiam libertatemque a barbaris vindicandam (Exhortation to take Italy and, avenging, free her from the barbarians)

Therefore, having considered all the things written above, and thinking to myself whether presently in Italy the times were running for honoring a new prince, and if there were the matter to give occasion to a prudent and virtuous one, to introduce therein the form[407] that might bring honor to him and good to the community of men in her, it appears to me that so many things concur to benefit a new prince that I do not know what time has ever been more apt for this. And if, as I said, in order to know Moses's virtue it was necessary that the people of Israel be slaves in Egypt, and to know the greatness of Cyrus's spirit, that the Persians be oppressed by the Medes, and to know the excellence of Theseus, that the Athenians be dispersed; so, at the present, in order to know the virtue of an Italian spirit, it was necessary that Italy reduce herself to the conditions in which she is at present, and that she were more slave than the Hebrews, more a servant than the Persians, more dispersed than the Athenians, without chief, without order, beaten, despoiled, torn, overrun, and having borne every sort of ruin. And even though up to now some gleam has shone in someone so that it might be possible to judge that he were ordained by God for her redemption, yet later it was seen that he was rejected by fortune in the highest course of his actions. So that, left as if lifeless, she waits for whomever might heal her wounds and put an end to the sacking of Lombardy, to the taxation of the kingdom and of Tuscany, and to heal her of her already long-festering sores. One sees how she prays God that he send her someone to redeem her from cruelties and barbarian insolences. One sees her also all ready and disposed to follow the flag, if only someone were to pick it up. Nor does one see at the present what she might hope in, more than in your illustrious house,

407. Note Machiavelli's ostentation of the Aristotelian dichotomy between matter and form.

which could put itself at the head of this redemption with her fortune and virtue, favored by God and by the Church of which it is now the prince. This is not too difficult, if you[408] summon up the actions and lives of the above-mentioned. And even though those men are rare and marvelous, nonetheless they were men, and each of those had lesser occasion than the present one: because their enterprise was not more just than this one, nor easier, nor was God more friend to them than to you.[409] Here is great justice: "War is just for those to whom it is necessary, and pious are arms when there is no hope except in them."[410] Here is very great potential; nor can there be great difficulty where there is great potential, provided that she[411] take up the orders of those I have proposed as models.[412] Beyond this, here one sees extraordinary things without precedent, delivered[413] by God: the sea has opened; a cloud has shown you the path; the rock has poured water; here manna has rained; everything has concurred in your greatness. The remainder you must do. God does not want to do everything, not to take from us free will and part of that glory which is our due.

And so it is no marvel if none of the afore-mentioned Italians has not been able to do what one can hope your illustrious house will do, and if in so many upheavals[414] in Italy, and in so many machinations of war, it always seems that military virtue in her is extinguished. This is because her old orders were not good, and there has been no one who has known how to find new ones: and nothing does so much honor to a man who newly arises as do the new laws and the new orders founded by him. These things have greatness in them when they are well founded, make him venerable and admirable, and in Italy matter is not lacking for the introduction of any form. Here is great virtue in the members, when it is not lacking in the heads.[415] Look how in duels and in the combats of the few, Italians are superior in

408. Plural or formal.

409. Plural or formal.

410. Livy IX, i.

411. The Medici house.

412. *Mira*, "aim" — models at which to aim. Recall the parable of the archer of Chap. III and recall the list of models: Moses, Cyrus, Hannibal, Cesare Borgia, Agathocles, et al.

413. Italian *condotti*, led. Here Machiavelli evokes the image of God as the supreme *condottiere*, and follows it with obvious humbug.

414. Italian *revoluzioni*, "revolutions."

415. Italian *capi*, also "chiefs."

strength, dexterity, and ingenuity. But when it comes to armies, they do not compare.[416] And all follows from the weakness of the chiefs;[417] because those who know are not obeyed, and each thinks he knows, since up to now there has not been anyone who has been able to raise himself by both virtue and fortune during so much time, in so many wars during the past twenty years;[418] when there has been a wholly Italian army, it has always given a bad account [of itself].[419] The first witness of this is the Taro,[420] thereafter Alexandria, Capua, Genoa, Vaila, Bologna, Mestre.

Therefore, if your illustrious house wants to follow those excellent men who redeemed their provinces, it is necessary above all things, as the true foundation of every enterprise, to provide oneself with one's own arms; because one can have neither more trusty nor truer nor better soldiers. And though each of them is good, all together they will come better, when they will see themselves commanded by their prince, and by him honored and favored. It is necessary therefore to prepare for oneself these arms in order to be able to defend oneself from foreigners with Italian virtue. And even though the Swiss and Spanish infantry are esteemed terrible, nonetheless there is a terrible defect in both, by means of which a third order could not only oppose them but be confident of overcoming them. Because the Spanish cannot withstand horse,[421] and the Swiss have to have fear of infantry, if in combat they meet any that prove as obstinate as they. That is why it has been seen, and will be seen by experience, that the Spanish are not able to withstand French cavalry, and the Swiss being ruined by the Spanish infantry. And, even though a complete experience of the latter has not been seen, *tamen*[422] a taste of it was seen on the day of Ravenna, when the Spanish infantries confronted the German battalions which serve under the same orders as the Swiss: where the Spaniards, with bodily agility and the help of

416. *Compariscono*, literally, "they don't show up."

417. *Capi*, also "heads."

418. I.e., since 1494.

419. Italian "*ha sempre fatto mala pruova*," literally, "has always made bad proof."

420. At Foronovo on the Taro River in 1495, Francesco Gonzago fought the retreating Charles VIII, who nonetheless made good his retreat. Alexandria was taken by the French in 1499, Capua in 1501, Genoa in 1507. Bologna was abandoned by the Papal Legate in 1511, and Mestre was burned by a Spanish commander in 1513. In 1509, Louis XII destroyed Venice's power on land.

421. I.e., they cannot bear up against cavalry.

422. Latin, even so.

their *brocchieri*[423] had come in under the pikes and were hurting them safely without the Germans having any remedy; and had not cavalry shocked them, they would have consumed them all. Therefore, the defect of both these infantries being known, one can ordain a new one, which might resist horses and not have fear of infantry; all of which the generation of armies and the changes of orders will accomplish. And these are among those things that, when newly ordained, give reputation and greatness to a new prince.

Thus, one must not let this occasion pass, so that Italy, after so much time, might see her redeemer. Nor can I express with how much love he would be received. In all the provinces which have suffered by these foreign[424] floods; with what thirst of vengeance, with what obstinate faith, with what piety, with what tears. How many doors would be closed to him? Which peoples would deny him obedience? What envy would be opposed to him? What Italian would deny him homage? This barbarian domination stinks to all. Let, therefore, your illustrious house take this undertaking with the spirit and with the hope with which just enterprises are taken up; so that, under her insignia, this fatherland may be ennobled by it, and under her auspices that saying of Petrarch may come true:

> Virtue against furor
> will take arms; and the fighting be short:
> for the ancient valor
> in Italian hearts is not yet dead.

---

423. Circular, shieldlike devices with a spike in the middle.

424. Italian *esterne*, external. Not necessarily non-Italian.

Rethinking *The Prince*

Machiavelli and Modernity

W. B. ALLEN

We are accustomed to think that liberal democracy protects society's weak against the strong and that it is based on honest public debates about the common good. It is remarkable, therefore, that so many of the architects of modern politics find Machiavelli's *Prince* a source of inspiration and that so many of them defended Machiavelli against adherents of religion and classical philosophy. But what can the advocates of modern democracy have in common with a book full of recipes for force and fraud? As we look more closely at the relationship between Machiavelli and modern democracy, we find that both stand on the same side of an argument as old as Western philosophy itself. Along with the opponents of Socrates, Machiavelli and the founders of modern democracy believe that to rule is not essentially to follow the laws of nature and reason but rather to succeed in asserting one's will over others. How the founders of modern democracy can derive the protection of the weak from naked will, from the notion that right is the interest of the stronger, how they defend Machiavelli and their own kinship with him, is worth examining. By way of contrast, it is also worthwhile to glance at some modern democrats whose relationship with Machiavelli is altogether different.

Consider the early British republican Henry Neville (1620–94). Writing a century after Machiavelli's death, Neville responded to the standard charges against the Italian, which he collapses into one, namely, that he finds no space for virtue or justice among men, except that pretending to be just or virtuous may be useful in the pursuit of power. Neville culminated his defense by putting the following passage into Machiavelli's mouth: "Whoever in his Empire is tyed to no other Rules than those of his own Will and Lust, must either be a Saint or else a very Devil incarnate; or if he be neither of these, both his Life and his Reign are like to be very short; for whosoever takes upon him so execrable an Employment as to rule Men against the Laws of Nature and of Reason, must turn all topsie turvy, and never stick at any thing, for if once he halt he will fall and never rise again."

Neville called this the "Christian Truth" and meant to give the impression that Machiavelli and himself, like Christians and classicists, believe that rulers must be bound by natural law rather than follow their own desires. Yet the alert reader notices that his passage is both very close in form to, and very different in substance from, a famous passage in Aristotle's *Politics*: "The man who is isolated—who is unable to share in the benefits of political association, or has no need to share because he is already self-sufficient—is no part of the polis, and must therefore be either a beast or a god. . . . Man, when perfected, is the best of animals; but if he be isolated from law and justice he is the worst of all. . . . That is why, if he be without virtue, he is a most unholy and savage being, and worse than all others in the indulgence of lust and gluttony. Justice [which is his salvation] belongs to the polis."

Neville did more than put a classical argument in Christian terms, supplanting the reference to a beast or a god with a reference to a saint or a devil. Aristotle had argued that the "polis is by nature" and that man is "perfected" within the polis. Most important, however, Aristotle's "worst animal" is worse because he is without virtue and therefore living only to satisfy "lust and gluttony." But Neville's "worst man" is worse precisely because the only way to succeed in his "will and lust" is to prevail over others with complete injustice: he "must never stick at any thing." That is, while for Aristotle "lust and gluttony" offer no prospect of human perfection, for Neville "lust and gluttony" can be perfected as instruments of rule so long as one totally disregards the demands of justice and never shrinks from any act required to get one's way. Neville's Machiavelli says that to "rule men against the Laws of Nature and Reason" is an "execrable" business. But we note that this originator of modern democracy believes violating nature and reason is just a business, and an eminently doable and profitable business at that. Neville's "isolated man" is by definition a ruler, and one who is isolated only insofar as he succeeds or fails in the assertion of an empire over others. Note well that he believes power is beyond good and evil.

Stated in this manner, the question that Neville succeeded in posing for Machiavelli by comparison with Aristotle is identical with the challenge of Glaucon and Adeimantus in Plato's *Republic*: that Socrates prove the superiority of justice to injustice even in the worst case, in which the justest of persons must endure the reputation for perfect injustice. The brothers had argued that only if he did this could Socrates refute Thrasymachus's accusation that justice is for the simpleminded who do not know enough to prefer their own interest over that of others. According to Thrasymachus, justice, properly speaking, is the right of the stronger — that is, force or injustice that succeeds; Thrasymachus's justice is Neville's "worst man" — the kind of man he finds perfectly natural.

This always was and remains the charge against Machiavelli, that he teaches the "means justifying the end" or, in Neville's words, that to succeed in ruling one must "never stick at any thing." Neville's fictitious defense of Machiavelli suggests that his own most comprehensive work, *Plato Redivivus*, was perhaps written with the same Machiavellian mentality. So if, as is likely, Neville's reborn Plato was Machiavelli, Neville's defense of liberal democracy has to be understood as founded on moral distinctions very different from those of Socrates. Hence the question: Is the "born again Plato" on whom Neville founds liberal democracy a dialectically superior Thrasymachus — in which case liberal democracy is founded on indifference to justice — or is there an alternative to the defense of justice that Plato placed in the mouth of Socrates? In that case, liberal democracy would be founded in superior claims to justice.

Neville's defense answered the charge that Machiavelli's (and his own) way of thinking instructs tyrants with the claim that *all* rulers rule without right. This, he says, is the condition of mankind after "the lust of our first Parents did at that time disappoint the good intention of God in making a pure world" and after the "Bishops of Rome . . . frustrated the merciful purpose [God] . . . intended for the World by his Son" eventuates in the "empire of will and lust." But if every possible regime must make light of moral virtue, by what standard would anyone choose among regimes? If all politics lowers men, and all organized churches are merely other forms of politics or other forms of self-seeking, none inherently better than the other, what opportunities exist for human elevation?

As we answer these questions, we must also try to distinguish the real Machiavelli from the image of him created by not a few founders of modern politics.

Appearance Is Everything

Our answers must begin with the fact that Machiavelli expressed no fundamental preference for certain regimes as against others. Because he does not discuss the moral advantages of regimes, the political science he creates is "value-free." For him, the role of morals in politics (one might almost say the role of words in general) is mainly to make useful impressions or, to put it starkly, to cultivate illusions. The only remaining question of principle is the extent to which "custom [ethics]" and "rule [force]" will enter into play for the sake of making the most effective impressions. It is the task of the prince, or indeed of any ruler in any regime whatever, to decide clearly when it will be more useful to emphasize force and when to emphasize ethos. This, then, is the center of Machiavellian thought: it reduces ethos to useful illusions.

If Machiavelli reduced ethics to illusion or appearances, why did he make it so plain to the readers of *The Prince*? How does widespread knowledge of the fact that politics is merely appearance and morality is mere pretense affect the few readers who are capable of ruling and the many who are not?

Leo Strauss observed that Machiavelli's *Prince* organizes all political discourse in terms of the relations between the prince and the multitude. The difference between the few and the many here is in terms not of relative power but of relative knowledge. Indeed, the preface to *The Prince* distinguishes between prince and people in terms of different perspectives and levels of knowledge. It seems that, for Machiavelli, power derives from these differences. Thus, even those who take Machiavelli's great work in its nominal terms as a manual for princes must nonetheless concede that though it addresses itself to the few, these few are defined not by birth or strength of arm but by their ability to pay attention to how differences in perspective make for power. So when Machiavelli writes in the Epistle Dedicatory that in order to know the nature of the people, it is best to be a prince and in order to know the nature of the prince, it is best to be of the people, he is not telling us that the multitudes have knowledge of princely things. Rather, Machiavelli's virtuosity lends insight to the few capable of absorbing it, thereby rendering them knowledgeable of politics and also of themselves. This is Machiavelli's version of the formula "know thyself," for which Socrates is famous. Both Socrates' injunction and Machiavelli's surrogate version imply the possibility of improving the lot of those who understand. But whereas Socrates' understanding leads to moral improvement, Machiavelli's leads to power.

What does Machiavelli's publication of the knowledge that morality is an illusion to be managed carefully do to the politics of those who follow him? How is liberal democracy shaped by consciousness of its foundation in amorality? Machiavelli would hardly have been surprised that this consciousness is not universal.

A Sun without Shadow

Consider when Machiavelli says that he will spurn imagined republics and principalities in order to pursue what is "known to be in reality," in order to avoid the certain ruin that would befall the few who could be good "in all things . . . among so many who are not good," he is doing something akin to what the philosopher in Plato's *Republic* did when he climbed out of the proverbial cave. The philosopher distinguishes himself from the multitude by freeing himself from the shadows on the wall of the cave, formed by artificial light illuminating man-made objects (conventions) and casting their shadows against the wall of a cave. After being dragged out of the cave, the philosopher gazes upon the pure light of the sun. When the philosopher-king lays down the laws for the just republic, he is presumably informed by the knowledge gained by gazing on the light of pure truth. This is the reality that Machiavelli calls "imaginary." Whether the truths of the sun or those of the cave are imaginary, they are obviously so different that those who live by one set cannot be ruled according to the other. Any philosopher-king must concern himself with the problems of ordinary people, who remain chained in the shadows of artificial light. For any political judgment to be acceptable to such people, it must proceed from the appearances created by the shadows within the cave. Accordingly, the philosopher-king is not free to rule by the pure light of the sun, a light that blinds one to shadows in direct proportion to the extent that one looks at it directly.

Socrates was not unaware of this difficulty and accordingly provided for a "noble lie," proceeding from the shadow world, to be taught to citizens in the just city. This Phoenician tale imputed the different capacities and functions of individuals to different metals (gold, silver, bronze) born in their souls. On the basis of this lie, men of different capacities could live together harmoniously. But can a philosopher-prince, can anyone, live with the "lie in the soul," that is, by repeating a mere convention, an appearance, the *verità effettuale*, while knowing it is only a convention — and while knowing that those who treat it as merely useful will benefit at the expense of those who believe it is true? Socrates held that the lie in the soul was the thing the philosopher per se could least tolerate. What happens when the prince, and all the readers of *The Prince*, live with Machiavelli's truth that politics is all appearance? At the very least, politics becomes the management of symbols in which fewer and fewer people believe. Gradually, the cloak of illusion falls, revealing naked force. Of course, not every would-be prince can manage illusions as well as every other. The winner, then, must be a special class of prince, the philosophically informed prince who most fully conforms to the Machiavellian standard. That standard, however, has no hint of the common good nor of protection of those who cannot protect themselves.

Because all politics, even in the best case, is dissimulation, it is no longer possible to distinguish the best rule from the worst rule by reference to regimes as such. Thus, because that state is best which is commanded by the best man, every state, including the republican, attains like success only as a matter of degree. But Machiavelli also tells us that a Borgia or an Agathocles can be an example of political virtue. Hence we ask: What, on Machiavellian grounds, can be meant by the terms "best man" and "worst man"? In what sense can states commanded by such paragons of virtue be good? Particular virtues having been jettisoned for the sake of the "sovereign virtue," namely, the capacity to succeed, do we not lose all ability to distinguish best and worst?

Machiavelli, following Thrasymachus's argument, could respond that even if some few could still recognize the best men, they would be unable to make them visible to the many, and the language they would use to discuss the best would echo nothing of the world of politics. If such good men were involved in politics, they would stand on the same ground as the worst men in the opinion of the multitude. When Machiavelli substituted for the Platonic distinction between truth and appearance (or nature and convention) the concept of *verità effettuale*, he applied his sovereign logic of success across the board to every political undertaking, including appearances or the manipulation of opinion. True, he made political efficacy depend on success in sustaining the passivity of the prince's clientele, but he did so from necessity. That is why one cannot stop at saying a prince can be loved by his people. Being loved by the people means to be thought just. For Machiavelli's best men, who rule as princes, to be thought just and to know themselves to be regarded so is to live with a lie in the soul. Conversely, insofar as the people understand the true nature of things, they can call their regime just only by living the same lie.

At the start of chapter XV of *The Prince*, Machiavelli "explicitly evacuated the moral question." Because the moral question has no citizenship in Machiavelli's world, whoever dares to pose it sincerely is profoundly subversive. What, then, is the practical meaning of justice in modern Machiavellian politics? When the prince or collectivity acts, it is as much liable to ill-doings as any private individual, because its motives are intensely private. Thus, every individual must be prepared to defend against the regime. In the clear, shining light emanating from Machiavelli's *Prince*, we can see through the other "noble lie" that later theorists, after Machiavelli, would call the transition from the state of nature to the state of civil society. Reality is this: individuals will care as deeply for themselves within society as they ever might have in any hypothetical state of nature. We can call the acts of any government just by the same standards we use in terming just the acts of private vengeance, namely, defensive notions of restraint, constraint, deterrence, and self-defense. This is the underlying reality that a prince must understand even as he tries to manipulate appearances.

Now, consider that Plato and Aristotle as well as the Christian tradition teach that political life must take its bearings from the transcendent, which is more real than the quotidian world of appearances, perceptions, and stimuli. Machiavelli's enthronement of appearances as the exhaustive description of things political necessarily foreshortened human horizons, creating a shadow-world deprived of light, a world in which politics emerges out of the communalizing of private vengeance.

The Just Return

Founded on the argument that all politics is appearances, Machiavelli's response to Glaucon-Adeimantus is on two levels. On the first level the response is identical to that of Thrasymachus. Chapter XVIII of *The Prince* declares that it is better to appear virtuous than to be virtuous, because the virtuous or just man labors under the disadvantage that the appearance of injustice is a political liability and because Machiavelli makes political success the ultimate standard. Because the title to rule is rather the appearance of justice than justice itself, the appearance of injustice defeats every title to rule. The challenge from Glaucon-Adeimantus, however, questioned not whether justice were more or less effective than injustice in politics. It questioned whether justice were better than injustice for the individual. Thus, a further response is required, this one involving Machiavelli's embrace of Thrasymachus, not as the best guide to effectiveness but as the best of men, simply.

To argue that the just man is better off, even when appearing unjust, one must deal with Socrates' claim that the best men rule only to avert rule by the worst men. If justice's failure to appear just results in the actual rule of the unjust, then the just must accustom themselves to the rule of the worst men, the fate Socrates reprehends. Moreover, such an eventuality would defeat the sense of responsibility that the best men have toward other men. Plato and Aristotle believed that the best men had to concern themselves with rule, because that was the only prospect, however tenuous, of bringing virtue to the lives of the many. The many, in their eyes, could not achieve the self-control that is the condition of virtue. In that formulation the classical authors tie the fates of the many to the prospects of political success by the few. By cutting the connection between rule and improvement in moral character, Machiavelli liberates the best from the many and leaves only the question of whether there are other reasons, or any reason at all, for the few to concern themselves with rule.

Once the obligation to act according to natural or divine standards is removed, the question that remains for the most able men is how to participate in the management of political appearances to secure their own interests. The very best of men, however, realize that their highest interest is to know things as they are rather than as they appear to be. The chief condition for the effective management of appearances is a knowledge of things as they are. Accordingly, while the few prevail in politics, they will enjoy the best opportunities to sustain their own interest in transcending everyday demands and in understanding the reality that is to be found there. But Machiavelli's understanding of reality is not conducive to improving their or anybody else's character. To what, then, is modern politics conducive?

Thrasymachus defined political justice as the "interest of the stronger"; he insisted that rulers rule in their own interests and not in the interest of the ruled. Socrates insisted that such rule would be possible only where the rulers had actual knowledge of the interest or good of the ruled. Shepherds, he maintained, can benefit from the sheep only by means of an art that looks to the good of the sheep. Similarly, rulers had to look to the good of the ruled even if their purpose is merely to preserve the ruled in a condition suitable to provide the rulers with the advantages rulers sought from them. Thrasymachus was willing to concede that. Machiavelli, however, maintains that the ruled are governed in their propensities to submit or to rebel by their opinions and that their opinions could be managed: it suffices for rulers to keep the ruled quiet ("abstain from their women") in order to reap the benefit they are after. Hence, Machiavelli's ruler wants more than the satisfaction of the lust and gluttony that seemed so important to Thrasymachus. Rather, he is interested in shutting out of the minds of the ruled the very notion that the regime they live under might be wrong. The right of the stronger, for Machiavelli, is to be unimpeded by the minds of the weaker.

The implications for liberal democracy are easy to perceive. Once individuals, families, religious groups, localities, guilds, lose the capacity to say to their ruler, "You cannot order me to deviate from what I am doing and make me do what you want because that is intrinsically wrong," the only title to rule is the force of greater numbers or force per se. Machiavelli overturned every moral claim to rule. In the vacuum that otherwise remained, he left only the dynamics of greater numbers, or *force majeure*. Because those greater numbers — and indeed armies — are to be managed through their opinions, however, it must also follow that the rule of the stronger will consist entirely of staging the opinions to be embraced by those who are less mentally tough.

Once government has been reduced to staging the opinions to be embraced by the multitude, every political calculation must have reference to those opinions. Although the language or the appearance of politics must invoke "rights" or the "common good" or earthly salvation, in fact all that is at stake is what the people imagine themselves to enjoy. Liberal democracy consists above all in fostering the enjoyments of the people (I mean that this is the explicit understanding of such regimes in the contemporary era), with an ever-watchful eye toward the emergence of claims and enjoyments by isolable groups or individuals that delegitimize the sharing of the regime's goods. The most threatening of all claims are moral claims, measuring what ought to be against what is. This is not new. Socrates stood out in, and threatened, ancient Athens precisely by raising such claims. That is why Athens killed him. Modern polities, shaped by Machiavelli, are even less tolerant of moral questions than was Athens.

Because liberal democracy, having eliminated all competing claims, takes the greater number as the only legitimate social force, it makes rule of the stronger its foundation. Indeed, this rule of the stronger is explicitly evoked as rule in its own interest. Karl Marx, in *Critique of the Gotha Programme*, argued correctly that because democracy is rule in the interest of the many as opposed to that of the few, the more a government, because democratic, represents an increasing proportion of the people the more oppressive it would become to the diminishing number of outsiders, even unto crushing them. So long as coherent opinion can be fashioned in a society, that society can be constituted as a liberal democracy according to the Thrasymachean principle of justice. This is Machiavelli's accomplishment.

Machiavelli did not produce this result on the grounds of the moral superiority of liberal democracy, nor on account of a view of human nature that sees liberal democracy as providing human fulfillment or perfection. Rather than subject the brightest and most willful men of any city, earthly or heavenly, to any law not of their own making, Machiavelli liberated them by giving them license to take as much power as they could, above all over moral claims. The prince speaks not from the point of view of justice (to which he could lay claim only through an act of submission to a law outside himself) but from the point of view of complete knowledge of his *verità* to which he must lay claim without submission. Thus did Machiavelli conquer the modern world — or at least most of it.

The United States

Is the United States a thoroughly liberal democracy on the Machiavellian model? When George Washington delivered his "Farewell Address," he took special pains to distinguish the American regime from all others of his time. The difference between the United States and the rest of the world was the basis of his argument against all "permanent alliances or enmities" with foreign states. Some at the time, and not a few since, took this position as pure Machiavellianism. But Washington was expressing something else: as a republic of equals, America would always lack the flexibility that allows independent princes to be one thing or to pursue one objective today and another tomorrow, sacrificing the interests of his subjects in pursuit of his own.

These reasons for America's restraint in foreign policy escaped the French minister to the United States. He described Washington's address as "a piece extolling ingratitude, showing it as a virtue necessary to the happiness of states, presenting interest as the only counsel which governments ought to follow in the course of their negotiations, putting aside honor and glory."

For Washington, however, interest was not the sovereign principle. That principle was the integrity of public opinion. In a free republic, public opinion could not change with the intricacies of policy. Accordingly, the free republic must operate so as never to sacrifice the public faith to expediency. That goal, in turn, is attainable only to the degree that the republic is parsimonious in pledging its faith. The only way to minimize that risk is to pursue interest (a matter of necessity) consistently "guided by justice." Washington identified a transcendent interest that would become the permanent basis of opinion in the republic. In doing so, he rejected the notion that opinion, once established, could be managed into any shape to fit whatever the rulers — or indeed the majority — happened to desire at any given time. A settled and permanent opinion — one not managed by the rulers but founded on natural and divine law — is the foundation of republican freedom in the United States.

How, then, did the United States once arrive at a defense of liberal republicanism independent of the Machiavellian foundation? Well before

Washington's farewell, John Adams had indicated the significance of this question: "Machiavelli was the first who revived the ancient politics. The best part of his writings he translated almost literally from Plato and Aristotle, without acknowledging the obligation; and the worst of sentiments, even in his *Prince*, he translated from Aristotle without throwing upon him the reproach. Montesquieu borrowed the best part of his book from Machiavel, without acknowledging the quotation." As our foregoing argument makes clear, we dissent from Adams's reading of Machiavelli. Nevertheless, he hints at some kind of relation between Machiavelli's moral skepticism and the American Revolution. We must ask further, therefore, whether and to what extent, George Washington notwithstanding, the United States is Machiavellian.

The first defense of the nation's liberal republicanism occurs in the Declaration of Independence. The core of this document is the axiom "All men are created equal," and its deduction, that legitimate governments derive their just powers from the consent of the governed. Although these principles are founded in the laws of nature and of nature's God, not even God may be conceived to provide forms of government for men by any agency other than their particular consent. I call this a form of moral skepticism not on account of any imagined limitation on God but on account of the limitation it imposes on man.

To understand the Declaration of Independence as a form of moral skepticism we must first abandon the notion that moral skepticism is somehow in opposition to morality. Second, we need to situate the claims of the Declaration amid comprehensive claims about the human condition. Plato and Aristotle first wrote of the relationship between morality and wisdom in politics. They did so in such a way as to make clear beyond every haggle that, however defective any given law may be, all law points to an independent standard of right. The deduction seems unavoidable that law or politics is legitimated in direct proportion to its approximation to right (as opposed to the weight of majority opinion).

Machiavelli, indeed, sundered the ligature between politics and right. Paradoxically, however, he was anything but indifferent to right. In fact, he cared even more about right than about politics. His charge against the ancients amounted to the case that they had enslaved or subordinated right (or truth or wisdom) to politics, to the disservice of truth and wisdom.

The ancients recognized distinctions between those who are capable of penetrating human things and those who can aspire no higher than to salutary opinions. Machiavelli accepted this distinction and regarded it as the most important human matter (*il principe e il popolo*). By the same token, he regarded as manifestly inequitable the ancients' insistence that the best men be subservient to the natural and divine ends of politics. He then opposed the ancients, not merely to save the best men from having to bow before ordinary virtue but also to emancipate the best souls from an enterprise that could indeed eventuate in decent, republican order but was unlikely to produce grandeur.

In summary, the moral problem stands thus: according to the ancients, those who are or may be wisest incur special obligations to approximate law to reason. The question Who shall rule? becomes a question about the best capacities to realize the intent of the natural law. Hence, reason or wisdom seems the only just title to rule. From a standard of right inherent in but beyond the city, the ancients arrived at a morality prior to politics and in the name of which politics could be shaped. The ancients saw the end of rule, wherever good rule was possible, as producing self-governing citizens. Rule was for the sake of the virtue of the citizens. Legitimate governments are governments in which good men, self-governing men, rule and produce others like themselves.

Here Machiavelli drew the line: virtue would no longer command the exertions of the best. All modern thinkers who have wanted to be free to think without regard to the constraints of natural and divine law are the fruits of the Machiavellian revolution.

This revolution, however, inadvertently tied the best men still more closely to political life: because ruling had become decisively instrumental (or value-free) and had no proper end of its own, rulers had to seek new modes of justifying what they were doing. Among the new principles put into play was the invention of an original state of nature. But ultimately a single device won general acceptance — namely, that the legitimacy of government depended on the consent of the governed. Consent is an especially convenient principle because it is value-free. Any other mechanism implied a species of moral persuasion, hence, ultimately tutoring in virtue (even if specious). Consent now became not what it was for Aristotle, decisive in a good regime, but decisive for politics altogether.

The principle of consent in the Declaration is substantially different. The main difference is that in almost all the formulations of the principle of consent that antedate the Declaration, men consent to the fact of government rather than to its specific form and powers. This is true even in Locke, for whom the whole consents to a government and the majority establishes it. The Declaration, by contrast, confronts directly the very question that animated Machiavelli's dialogue with the ancients: Who has just title to rule? The Declaration's answer is that ordinary people (insofar as the many are ordinary) shall rule. The people who approved the Declaration believed that far more people were capable of self-government than was ever conceded by Machiavelli and the ancients. Indeed, they believed that most people may be so capable. The Declaration does not recognize any special privileges for the best souls.

Nevertheless, the Declaration is not an anathema against the best. But the best were not to be exempted from the spirit of obedience to the laws. The claim that no one man is by nature the ruler of any other amounted to a denial that any of the various superiorities and inferiorities among men could in themselves determine the foundations of polity or morality. The authors of the Declaration conceded that wisdom, virtue, or inspiration deserve deference, but not to the point of imposing the will of a superior on that of any other man. The practical consequence is that the founders departed from Machiavelli's regard for the most efficacious as much as they did from the ancients' respect for the best.

The Declaration's consent reposes on the obligation, incumbent on all humans, not just the best, to observe natural right and practice reason. Thus the Declaration imposes moral persuasion as the only legitimate ground of polity. That, in turn, makes sense to the extent that each person governs his or her own passions (however imperfectly) and makes that governance the comprehensive moral foundation of political life. This powerful focus on human weakness and fallibility is skepticism — not about morality per se but about the status to be accorded all competing moral claims, even true claims, asserted by human beings. It is as if the founders believed that the decent political life is accessible only by labored, repetitious striving for virtuous consensus by a virtuous people in every instance, from birth to death. How do people draw virtue from the contemplation of their imperfections? That is the non-Machiavellian question to which George Washington provided his distinctly non-Machiavellian response in the "Farewell Address."

Machiavelli's Realism

CARNES LORD

That Machiavelli brought a new realism to the study of politics is undeniable. Machiavelli deserves to be considered the earliest, most forceful, and most influential exponent of the style of statecraft that would become known in later ages as realpolitik, defined as an approach to politics rooted in a cynical view of human motives and possibilities, and devoted to advancing the interests of a state without regard for moral or religious strictures.

Machiavelli's *Prince* is generally considered the classic statement of such an approach to politics. Not published until after its author's death, in 1527, *The Prince* came at once under vigorous attack and was banned by the Catholic Church. Perhaps in part because of the underground status it long enjoyed, *The Prince* soon became if not the most famous, certainly the most infamous book of its kind ever written, while its author became a stock villain in drama and an image of the Antichrist incarnate. In the eighteenth century, Frederick the Great — himself no innocent in the pursuit of power through blood and iron — could make this assessment of the book: "I have always considered Machiavelli's *Prince* as one of the most dangerous works ever to be disseminated in the world. It is a book which falls naturally into the hands of princes and of those with a taste for politics. Since it is very easy for an ambitious young man, whose heart and judgment are not sufficiently developed to distinguish clearly between good and evil, to be corrupted by maxims which flatter the impetuosity of his passions, any book which can contribute to this must be regarded as absolutely pernicious and contrary to the good of mankind."[1]

It is fashionable today to consider judgments of this kind naive and misleading. Yet they capture a critical dimension of Machiavelli's great book, and of his thought generally, that too often disappears in the bland reinterpretations of contemporary scholars. Not only does Machiavelli shock (and there is much in *The Prince* to shock even contemporary readers), but he *intends* to shock. Once one realizes this, one is in a position to begin to appreciate what is truly original and significant in Machiavelli's thought. Hence, Machiavelli's "realism" must eventually be understood less as a straightforward method of political analysis than as a kind of rhetorical strategy, a highly self-conscious attempt to alter the very terms of contemporary political discourse.[2]

Today Machiavelli is variously said to be the founder of modern nationalism and (or) of the modern concept of the state; the founder or an important precursor of modern social science understood as the realistic, empirical, and value-neutral study of man and society; and — most recently and fashionably — a founder or important early representative of the tradition of modern civic republicanism.

These claims cannot be fully evaluated here. It would not be difficult, however, to show that each of them is to some degree problematic in its own terms. The Florentine or Italian nationalism conspicuous in the final chapter of *The Prince* did not lack for influential antecedents; it is also thoroughly undercut by the advice to foreigners that Machiavelli freely dispenses elsewhere in the book concerning the best approach to take in conquering what he (in a linguistic reminiscence of imperial Rome) calls the "province" of Italy. At the same time, there is little evidence that Machiavelli succeeded — or indeed was especially interested — in developing an impersonal concept of the "state" along modern lines.[3]

Did Machiavelli then originate an "empirical" approach to politics, that is, one that declines to make evaluative assessments of men's political behavior as well as recommendations for action? To the contrary. Machiavelli's writings are shot through with what most social scientists today would consider insupportable value judgments and unwarranted generalizations. Moreover, Machiavelli repeatedly stresses his intention to benefit human life rather than simply analyze men's political behavior. In both respects, he is much closer to the political science of classical antiquity than he is to contemporary social science.[4] What then are his preferences?

Machiavelli's political science is not coextensive with the teaching of *The Prince*. Machiavelli's other great work, the *Discourses on the First Ten Books of Titus Livy*, presents the ancient Roman republic as the model of a well-ordered polity, and discusses political phenomena from the point of view of republics as distinct from princes. It is now generally accepted that Machiavelli maintained an attachment to the ideal of republican government throughout his career. In recent scholarship, Machiavelli's republicanism has increasingly come to be understood as the core of his contribution to modern political thought.[5]

And yet it is far from clear that Machiavelli's republicanism affords the proper point of entry into his thought as a whole, or accounts for its true distinctiveness. The tradition of Florentine republicanism, rooted as it was in the medieval and classical past, remained powerful in Machiavelli's day; but it was not primarily to this tradition that Machiavelli pointed his readers. Nor was he attracted by Venice, the other contemporary Italian state with long experience of republican political life — in spite of the fact that the Venetian government was much admired by many of the Florentine aristocrats in whose circle he moved. Machiavelli rarely refers to the humanist writers and statesmen who had articulated and defended the idea of republican government during the previous century or so. Instead, he turned to ancient Rome. We must try to appreciate the significance of this cardinal fact.

At the beginning of the *Discourses*, Machiavelli emphasizes the novelty of his enterprise. Presenting himself as a kind of Columbus traversing uncharted seas, he claims to have set out in search of "new modes and orders" and entered upon a "new way, as yet untrodden by anyone else." That this journey into a new world leads Machiavelli back to ancient times is only an apparent paradox. Machiavelli's contemporaries, so quick to admire ancient achievements in the arts and other areas, neglected the political achievements of the ancient world because they believed them difficult or impossible to imitate. They did so above all, he suggests, because they believed that what Machiavelli is pleased to call "the present religion" had fundamentally altered the condition of human life.[6]

Machiavelli's preference for ancient Rome evidently reflects more than an interest in classical republicanism as such. It rests on a thorough critique of Christianity as a set of beliefs and as a way of life. In the famous fifteenth chapter of *The Prince*, Machiavelli states his claim to originality in a way that leaves no doubt about his fundamental intention. Claiming that in discussing princely government he departs "from the order of others," Machiavelli there says that he will "go directly to the effective truth of the thing rather than its imagination" — for "many have imagined for themselves republics and principalities which no one has ever seen nor known to be in reality." The effectual truth Machiavelli has in mind is the ineffectuality of goodness or virtue as conventionally understood.

Machiavelli's new view takes its bearings, he tells us in this context, from "how men live" rather than "how they should live." This quintessential statement of Machiavellian "realism" is often misunderstood as somehow prefiguring the contemporary distinction between "facts" and "values," and hence as evidence of Machiavelli's commitment to "empiricism." In actuality, it is a powerful assertion of value, achieved by dramatically depicting the consequences of neglecting the ordinary interests and necessities of human life in this world in the name of a higher or otherworldly standard of virtue. As such, Machiavelli's distinction constitutes a frontal challenge not merely to conventional treatments of monarchic government (the "mirror of princes" literature) but also and more fundamentally to the moral outlook of the Christian tradition generally. At the same time, it declares war equally (if less emphatically) on the moral and political teaching of the classical philosophical tradition, a tradition which — primarily in its Aristotelian version — had been powerfully revived in the century and a half preceding Machiavelli and was widely seen as an important intellectual ally of Christian faith.

What precisely is the basis of Machiavelli's challenge to Christian morality? In the first half of *The Prince*, Machiavelli develops a notion of *virtù* that is intended to supplant the traditional accounts of moral virtue or human excellence available in the classical as well as the Christian tradition. Machiavelli's alternative account emphasizes the aspects of *virtu* that have to do with manliness, daring, and courage. Thus he makes virtue appear not as the good order of the soul, in the manner of the traditional teachings, but rather as a mere instrument for acquiring and enjoying the "good things of life" in the vulgar sense of that term.

At the level of politics, which remains in the foreground of his analysis, Machiavelli asserts that princely acquisitiveness is a "natural and ordinary desire," and proceeds to show that it is not necessarily incompatible with the satisfaction of ordinary men or the good order of the state. The "virtuous" prince in the new and true sense of the term is one who recognizes the imperative of aggrandizement at the expense of others and does whatever is necessary to secure both himself and his country against foreign threats. Accordingly, he points to military force as the primary element of statecraft. Therefore, Machiavelli tells us, the state must be founded both on "good laws" and on "good arms." But since "there cannot be good laws where there are not good arms, and where there are good arms there must be good laws," the prince can dispense with study of laws. That is to say, so long as the prince pays attention to Machiavelli's teachings about military force, he can dispense with what is arguably the central concern of classical as well as Christian political philosophy.

This same thought also helps explain Machiavelli's preference, as expressed particularly in the opening chapters of the *Discourses*, for acquisitive or expansionist Rome over competing models of republican government (notably, ancient Sparta and contemporary Venice, for which expansion was not the driving force). The successful prince or republic is one whose state is well armed for war and oriented toward expansion. The example of Rome is of special importance because it shows that power comes through the cultivation and practice of military virtue by an entire society, rather than by reliance on mercenary soldiers — the specific disease of the Italian republics of Machiavelli's own day. A prince or republic should rely not just on arms but on arms that belong to them. The mark of the competent prince or political leader is reliance on "one's own arms" as opposed to "the arms of others." Such people rule thanks to their own "virtue" rather than depending essentially on others or on "fortune." [7]

The full bearing of this advice becomes apparent only at the beginning of Chapter XXV, where Machiavelli disputes the common opinion that "worldly things are so governed by fortune and by God, that men cannot correct them with their prudence, indeed that they have no remedy at all." For Machiavelli, princes — and men generally — can devise remedies for what were traditionally considered the inherent limitations and disabilities of the human condition. Men can conquer their own fortune by relying on their own virtue rather than passively entrusting their salvation to powers external to themselves. In Machiavelli's famous formulation, fortune is to be seen no longer as an aloof and implacable deity, but as a woman who allows herself to be mastered by the ardent and impetuous young. [8]

But Machiavelli's rehabilitation of war and of the manly virtues associated with it by no means exhausts his challenge to the Christian outlook. In the course of his discussion of *virtu* in Chapter VI, Machiavelli states that "armed prophets" always succeed, "while the unarmed ones come to ruin." The ostensible reference is to Fra Girolamo Savonarola, the priest who dominated Florentine politics at the end of the fifteenth century but eventually fell from popular favor and was burned at the stake. Yet no one writing or reading such a passage could help thinking of Jesus, whose conquest of a whole civilization had not depended on force. Machiavelli knew full well that, from late Roman times to his own era, the political strength of Christianity had rested at least as much on its intrinsic appeal as on the sword wielded by Christian princes. How to account for the success of "unarmed prophecy" in its most important historical manifestation is perhaps *the* central puzzle of *The Prince*, if not of Machiavelli's political writings generally. The subject must remain a puzzle because he does not deal with it directly.

Part of the reason for this has to do with the nature of Machiavelli's own enterprise. It is not accidental that Machiavelli's famous peroration on the future of Italy at the end of *The Prince* adopts the tones and cadences of biblical prophecy. Machiavelli too is a kind of unarmed prophet. Lacking all power (as he reminds us in the Epistle Dedicatory of *The Prince*), yet wishing to use his knowledge for the benefit of humanity, Machiavelli understood that he had to become a student and imitator of the secular success of the Christian message. Machiavelli's "realism," then, is something quite different — and in many ways more adequate to the phenomena with which it deals — than the "realism" of contemporary international relations theory, with its emphasis on value-free models. For Machiavelli, the "effective truth" of human things cannot be understood simply in terms of material wants or needs, of acquisition or security in the ordinary sense of those words. Just as Machiavelli was more alive than his modern successors to the reality of honor and glory as motives of action in (at least the most interesting and formidable) political men, so he recognized the power of ideals to shape political behavior generally. He understood that the political and military realities of the world had been decisively affected by the victory of Christianity over paganism. His appreciation of this fact explains much of what is otherwise opaque in his writings and points the way to a proper understanding of the literary strategy that informs them.

In the second half of *The Prince*, Machiavelli presents us with his analysis of the fundamental appeal of Christianity and provides a sketch of what one may call his countertheology.[9] The key to this discussion is the emergence of the notion that "fraud" is fully equal if not superior to "force" as a requirement of princely success. For Machiavelli, Christianity is the extreme and therefore paradigmatic case of successful fraud in politics. The Christian religion attempts to hold men to impossible standards of behavior through the promise of rewards and punishments that are (he assumes) impossible of delivery. Yet the promise is highly effective — up to a point — in attaching men's loyalties to the princes of the Church and the secular rulers who depend on them. But the inevitable failure — or, better, the lack of evident success — in delivering heavenly goods and sanctions is in the end doubly corrupting, and hence destructive, of sensible politics.

Machiavelli illustrates the general point in Chapter XVII with reference to pity or compassion (*pietà*), the Christian virtue par excellence. Because men are naturally selfish and quarrelsome, a politics of compassion not only fails to maintain the good order of society but must eventually require restorative measures of extraordinary harshness. Thus Machiavelli's Florentines, "to escape a name for cruelty," allow their subject city of Pistoia to destroy itself in factional strife. By contrast, the notoriously ruthless Cesare Borgia restored order to the Romagna, a province under the nominal authority of the papacy, "united it, and reduced it to peace and *fede*," literally, "faith."

Machiavelli concludes that it is better for a prince to be feared than loved. But he makes clear that the fear instilled by what he calls "cruelty well used" is not necessarily incompatible with love in a certain sense of the term. Provided a prince avoids laying hands on the women or the property of his subjects, the harsh measures he takes to preserve public order will be accepted and, indeed, welcomed by those who stand to benefit from them. Ultimately, they will forge bonds of loyalty to the prince that will prove to be enduring, just as the Romagna held out for Borgia following the collapse of his sanguinary empire.

Machiavelli's argument—the message that is intended to improve on and eventually supplant the Christian message—may be summarized as follows. Men's natural desire to acquire must be respected as the premise of all political action. This desire cannot and should not be repressed. But it must be regulated so as to promote the common good. Such regulation is to be achieved not through moral exhortation but through political institutions with teeth—that is, institutions that both provide ordinary checks and balances to control contending social interests, and at the same time facilitate the application of extraordinary measures when necessary to surmount domestic or external crises. To say that for Machiavelli fear replaces love as the primary motive or guarantor of social order is true, but it is insufficient. In another and more fundamental sense: Machiavelli replaces Christian love—or, better, the combination of fear and love that appears in traditional Christian attitudes toward God—with his own combination of secular fear and love. For Machiavelli, men freed from religious passions are bound to love a prince who respects the necessities their own nature imposes on them; yet they require an authority that is more immediately and visibly fearful than the Christian God to check their unruly natural passions.

Machiavelli's barely concealed challenge to Christianity shocked contemporary opinion; that it did so, however, was anything but incidental to Machiavelli's intention. Machiavelli's irreverence, frivolous though it may sometimes appear, served the serious purpose of preparing the ground for the emergence of a public philosophy or ideology that could contend with Christianity as the basis of modern politics. Christian politics, which named and perfected (if it did not invent) the tool of "propaganda," could be countered effectively only on the level of ideas. From this point of view, Machiavelli must be regarded as the originator of the intellectual movement that would become known to later centuries as the "Enlightenment." His powerful rhetoric aimed to educate princes or potential princes, and through them peoples, regarding a "new way" of conceiving politics that would redound to the ultimate benefit of humanity as a whole.

At the level of politics as such, Machiavelli's thought points in two divergent directions, reflecting the ambivalence of his commitment to republicanism as traditionally understood. Machiavelli was the first great thinker to take his bearings not from the requirements of ordinary political life but from the extraordinary moment in politics — from civil disorder, conspiracies, coups, the founding of new regimes. For Machiavelli, republican or constitutional government could only be understood against the backdrop of the extraconstitutional action of extraordinary men — "princes" in the larger sense of the term — who alone are capable of establishing political orders and of renewing them when they have fallen into decay.[10] Hence Machiavelli must surely be granted his due as a seminal figure in the development of modern republican political thought. His emphasis on the importance of institutions as opposed to education in sustaining free government made its mark on the thought of Locke, Montesquieu, Hume, and the American founders. At the same time, Machiavelli must also be seen as a key figure in the development of the secular revolutionary tradition of modern times. Machiavelli's secularized version of the Christian synthesis of "love" and "fear" looks forward unmistakably to the ideological formula of modern totalitarianism. The Italian communist Antonio Gramsci saw clearly the revolutionary implications of Machiavelli's overall thought and understood the hidden kinship between Machiavelli's prince and the "modern prince" embodied by the Communist Party.[11] From this point of view, Machiavelli, more than any other figure, can claim to be the founder of modern politics *tout court.*

That there is much of enduring value in Machiavelli's political science will be very generally agreed. Yet it must also be said that few of Machiavelli's contemporary admirers have come fully to grips with the dependence of Machiavelli's teaching as a whole on the amoral if not immoral premises of his thought, which are as offensive to contemporary sensibilities as they were to those of Machiavelli's own day. Machiavelli can indeed be read as a refreshing corrective to the sentimentality, moralism, and cant of much contemporary commentary on politics. At the same time, our own recent experience — the collapse of the Communist experiment under the weight of the brutality and stupefying corruption of the Soviet system, not to speak of the continuing decline of culture, society, and constitutional order in the United States and throughout much of the West — forces us to wonder whether Machiavelli's attempt to expel morality from politics was as necessary or sensible as many today appear to believe.

Because all of us today are, in a sense, Machiavellians, it is difficult to gain the necessary perspective on the specific character and limitation of Machiavellian realism. Surely, though, Machiavelli's debunking of the traditional — Christian or classical — notion of virtue as the good order of the soul has left an enduring legacy of cynicism and self-indulgence against which our contemporary forms of piety seem increasingly powerless.

Machiavelli's insistence that men esteem their fatherland more than their soul, far from preparing the ground for the permanent extrusion of religious passion from politics and a revived civic virtue in the spirit of the ancient republics, seems rather to have given the impetus to our peculiarly modern combination of rootless individualism on the one hand and a dangerously obscurantist communitarianism — secular as well as religious — on the other.

One may argue that Machiavelli was not overly concerned with the problem of moral and political corruption because he envisioned periodic revolutionary upheavals that would sweep away entrenched elites and renew the fundamental fear that is the basis of all social order.[12] Such a notion — echoed in not so distant times by figures as diverse as Thomas Jefferson and Georges Sorel — seems today to lack all plausibility. Perhaps because his thought was so focused on the extreme rather than the everyday, Machiavelli seems to have overestimated both the appeal and the effectiveness of a statecraft based on blood and iron. If the Soviet Union, a regime built on blood and sustained by iron, could collapse under the weight of its own corruption and loss of moral legitimacy without stimulating any significant reaction from an army that was the most powerful in the world at the time, something would appear to be wrong with Machiavelli's premises. In fact, Machiavelli's emphasis in *The Prince* on arms or military prowess as the core of statecraft seems unsustainable in the last analysis. Even taking account of Machiavelli's revision of his own argument, especially in the last chapter of the book, it is difficult to avoid concluding that he succumbed in this instance to a pseudorealism inspired by his immediate historical situation.

Machiavelli's assertion that "arms" are the parents of "laws" is plainly true on a certain level. Nonetheless, as one surveys the modern world as a whole, there can be little doubt that Machiavelli's formulations had much less *direct* historical impact than those, for example, of John Locke, who couched an arguably Machiavellian teaching in the language of Christian natural law. Always and everywhere, one is tempted to say, law is more respectable than force — because, and to the extent that, man is a being with natural awareness of moral constraints. The fundamental failure of Machiavellian realism lies in its disregard of this truth.

NOTES

1. Frederick of Prussia, *Anti-Machiavel*, trans. Paul Sonnino (Athens, Ohio, 1981), p. 31.

2. For a recent protest against current Machiavelli scholarship along similar lines, see Mark Hulliung, *Citizen Machiavelli* (Princeton, 1983).

3. See Harvey C. Mansfield, Jr., "On the Impersonality of the Modern State: A Comment on Machiavelli's Use of *Stato*," *American Political Science Review* 77 (1983), pp. 849–57.

4. Consider Harvey C. Mansfield, Jr., "Machiavelli's Political Science," *American Political Science Review* 75 (1981), pp. 293–305. See, more generally, Leo Strauss, *Thoughts on Machiavelli* (Glencoe, Ill., 1985).

5. The most influential statement of this view is J. G. A. Pocock, *The Machiavellian Moment* (Princeton, 1975).

6. When Machiavelli says that neglect of the political lessons of antiquity "is due in my opinion not so much to the weak state to which the religion of today has brought the world, or to the evil wrought in many provinces and cities of Christendom by ambition conjoined with idleness, as to the lack of a proper appreciation of history, owing to people failing to realize the significance of what they read, and to their having no taste for the delicacies it comprises" (*Discourses* I, preface, ed. Bernard Crick [Harmondsworth, England, 1970], p. 98), he virtually forces the reader to complete the thought just indicated. This combination of boldness and reticence is characteristic of Machiavelli's writing.

7. *The Prince* VI.

8. *The Prince* XXV, end.

9. To claim that Machiavelli's critique of Christianity rests on a fully developed theology or metaphysics would be going too far; but it is equally wrong to overlook the many indications of interest in these matters found throughout his writings. See Strauss, *Thoughts on Machiavelli*, pp. 174–230, as well as Anthony J. Parel, *The Machiavellian Cosmos* (New Haven, 1992).

10. For this (neglected) dimension of Machiavelli's thought, see especially Gabreil Naudé, *Considérations politiques sur les Coups d'Estat* (Political considerations concerning coups d'état, 1639), a treatise of Machiavellian inspiration devoted to the analysis of extraconstitutional action broadly understood. An account of this work may be found in Friedrich Meincke, *Machiavellism: The Doctrine of Raison d'Etat and Its Place in Modern History*, trans. Douglass Scott (New Haven, 1957), chap. 7.

11. Antonio Gramsci, *Note sul Machiavelli*, translated by Louis Marks as *The Modern Prince* (New York, 1959).

12. *Discourses on Livy* III:1.

Machiavelli and America

HADLEY ARKES

Leo Strauss remarked that we would not "shock" anyone, that "we shall merely expose ourselves to good-natured or any rate harmless ridicule, if we profess ourselves inclined to the old-fashioned and simple opinion according to which Machiavelli was a teacher of evil." There would be no shock, because the intellectual classes in America had long since absorbed the premises deeply planted by Machiavelli. Those premises, and those teachings, contained, as Strauss wrote, the "maxims of public and private gangsterism": "What other description would fit a man who teaches lessons like these: princes ought to exterminate the families of rulers whose territory they wish to possess securely; princes ought to murder their opponents rather than to confiscate their property since those who have been robbed, but not those who are dead, can think of revenge; men forget the murder of their fathers sooner than the loss of their patrimony; true liberality consists in being stingy with one's own property and in being generous with what belongs to others; not virtue but the prudent use of virtue and vice leads to happiness . . . "?[1]

These maxims would no longer startle, because they have been incorporated in our sense of "political realism" or of how the world works. With a knowing wink and a wry smile, we hear that people are not barred from voting in Chicago because they have suffered the inconvenience of dying. Thus domesticated, this seamier side of politics now has become a subject fit for discussion. It was not always so. People in an earlier age were not unaware that in politics even good men may have to dirty their hands. But there seemed to be a code among the worldly to absorb that understanding of politics, while avoiding any temptation to celebrate it, or savor it, to make it the object of public discussion or any part of a "science" of politics, much less its central feature. Strauss came to the edge of this code when he noted that statesmen in constitutional orders may have to resort to measures beyond the strict rules of constitutionalism. But then, in a suggestive passage, Strauss held back overly explicit details: "Let us leave these sad exigencies," he wrote, "covered with the veil with which they are justly covered."[2]

Strauss was well aware that this sensibility was quickly receding from the modern period. And yet he also thought that the ideas that undergird this sensibility had been incorporated in the very character of the United States of America, the preeminently "modern" regime, the one that heralded itself as *novus ordo seculorum*, as something entirely new under the sun. Strauss contended that the United States "may be said to be the only country in the world which was founded in explicit opposition to Machiavellian principles."[3]

Indeed, the Declaration of Independence was the constitutive act by which the American states articulated the central principle of the republic. As Lincoln said at Gettysburg, the new nation was "brought forth," "conceived in liberty," and dedicated to the "proposition that all men are created equal." This proposition, Lincoln said, is the "father of all moral principles among us." The moral understanding of the American founders was reflected in that document; but it was also expressed in other writings of the founders, especially those who reflected most deeply on the "first principles" of the political order, James Wilson and Alexander Hamilton.

One commentator aptly remarked that Machiavelli taught us to take a posture of detachment in the face of vice. That posture was translated into the characteristic operating procedure of social science: to describe with precision what political men do, while abstaining from any moral judgment about their acts. Thus, social science has purged its language. A familiar, ancient word, *tyrant*, had been used not merely to describe but to cast a moral judgment: a tyranny was the corrupted, wrongful form of rule by one rightful monarch. Traditional language reflected the recognition that morality, and moral judgment, are as much part of our world as rocks and trees, and that to "describe" a Hitler or Stalin with the same label attached, say, to Frederick the Great would be to describe them falsely. But in the 1930s social science referred to Hitler and Stalin as "dictators" for the sake precisely of removing those moral shadings. And when "dictator" began to acquire all the sense of a deep pejorative, social science replaced it with the blander term "leader," as in the familiar accounts of Leonid Brezhnev and the Russian tyrants as "Soviet leaders."

Anyone attentive to these deliberate attempts to sift moral judgments out of the language of politics could not fail to notice how different is the style of the Declaration of Independence. That is because its drafters sought to avert, at every turn, the kind of misunderstanding that leads people to discuss the "powers" of government without discriminating between rightful and wrongful powers. In Madison's words, governments were made for "moral agents," for human beings who could reason about right and wrong.

In the same way, the drafters of the Declaration understood that the case for government began with certain axioms or "self-evident" truths grounded in nature of human beings: that because "all men are created equal," it is wrong to rule other humans in the way that men rule dogs and horses; and therefore that governments "derive their just powers from the consent of the governed." The drafters were evidently not explaining how governments came about in the style of social science. They knew fully well, as Hamilton would explain later, in the *Federalist* 1, that most governments come into being through force and accident and that they are sustained mainly by brute power. But the founders began by refusing to accept any "analytical" account of the authority of government that would abstract from the moral conditions on which legitimate authority is constituted.

Yet in doing so they were refusing to join a tendency that had already taken root in English law, and especially in international law, to identify legitimate authority with the government that simply held control of any territory as a matter of brute fact. That common modern understanding located the fount of authority simply in a sovereign, who was in a position to issue commands that would be obeyed as "law."

No teachings on jurisprudence were known more widely in America in the 1770s than the *Commentaries* of William Blackstone, who thought it was a "chimera" to refer to an unjust law. For Blackstone, it was incoherent to argue, in a court provided by the king, that the king's law was unjust and therefore not truly lawful in the deepest sense. That is because the king's very sovereignty provided the authority that attached to the courts of law in the first place, as well as to the remedies that would be handed down by judges. For judges to call into question the authority that gave force to their own judgments was to reduce their judgments — as Hobbes put it — to mere "words or breath," without legal meaning.

Thus Blackstone could regard it as solecism on the part of Locke to contend that "there remains still inherent in the people, a supreme power to alter the legislative, when they find the legislative act contrary to the trust reposed in them; for when such trust is abused, it is thereby forfeited."[4] To Blackstone, this was a careless mode of writing the principle of revolution into the standing law. Any meretricious mingling of that kind would work, inescapably, to the dissolution of the law: "However just this conclusion may be in theory, we cannot admit it, nor argue from it, under any dispensation of government, at present actually existing. For this devolution of power to the people at large, includes a dissolution of the whole form of government established by that people; reduces all the members to their original state of equality; and, by annihilating the sovereign power, repeals all positive laws whatsoever before enacted. No human laws will therefore suppose a case, which at once must destroy all law, and compel men to build afresh upon a new foundation; nor will they make provision for so desperate an event, as must render all legal provisions ineffectual."[5]

James Wilson, one of the original members of the United States Supreme Court, would cite this passage in his inaugural lecture as professor at the College of Philadelphia in 1790. His was the first appointment to a chair in law since the founding of the new Constitution, and this first lecture on jurisprudence was delivered in the presence of President Washington and Vice President Adams. Wilson took the occasion to pronounce certain first principles of American law, principally to reject Blackstone's teaching at the root. What Blackstone regarded as a "chimera," as a doctrine of profound incoherence, Wilson regarded as eminently plausible and part of the very foundation of American law. He explained that revolution "certainly is, and certainly should be taught as a principle for the constitution of the United States, and of every State in the Union."[6]

Even Blackstone admitted that the British revolution of 1688 had been legitimate. But, asked Wilson, what conditions had justified that revolution? Would not the English "constitution" then incorporate an awareness of the conditions on which the legally constituted government of the day might lawfully be deposed? Blackstone insisted that three conditions had to be met as a "conjunction of circumstances" to replicate the justification for the revolution of 1688. Wilson recalled them: "1. An endeavor to subvert the constitution, by breaking the original contract between the king and people. 2. Violation of the fundamental laws. 3. Withdrawing out of the kingdom."[7]

With more finickiness than principle, Blackstone had insisted that all three conditions be present or "the precedent would fail us." But the conjunction of the three merely described the story of James II in 1688, and bore no necessary relevance to principle. Let us suppose, Wilson said, that there was a monarch bent on subverting the fundamental laws. A monarch who sought to overturn the "original contract" between king and people and to place himself outside the laws would be putting himself at war with the people and the laws. But suppose this monarch proved hapless in the project. Suppose he had not the wit even to remove himself from the territory, as James II had done. Would the subversion of the law be any less? Would the monarch have been any less at war with the laws?[8]

Blackstone's maze of conditions sought to obscure this rudimentary but momentous point: it is indeed possible that anyone vested with sovereign authority could offend the deepest principles of lawfulness. They might kill without justification, injure people without regard for innocence and guilt, and they might do this for no purpose other than their own arbitrary power as an end in itself. Such a sovereign could be called a "lawless king" without any offense to logic.

Wilson, in this first opinion on the Supreme Court, had already taught that law in America stood on a different foundation from law in England. Now he offered to his prospective students George Washington and John Adams the following anchoring axioms of the new jurisprudence in America: that people in sovereign office might well perform unjustified and therefore lawless acts; that those acts could not be cleansed of their lawless attributes by the fact that their perpetrators were wrapped in the mantle of office. Such acts, though invested with "legal" authority, could not rightfully claim nor elicit from the people an obligation to obey. In America, at least, the modern maxim that "the Sovereign can do no wrong" was to be treated as a matter of convenience for the powerful, nothing more than a noxious fable.

To recognize that the sovereign may indeed be lawless — and that the law itself had to make a place for this recognition — was true political realism and sobriety. It did not mark, as Wilson suggested, a willingness to infuse romance into the law, but a truer willingness to take the world as it is. All of this presupposed, of course, that "principles of law" do not depend for their validity on the men who hold official power at any given time. Only against the enduring principle of lawfulness could one measure the acts of a sovereign and find him to be a "lawless sovereign."

During the Constitutional Convention in Philadelphia, Wilson and Oliver Ellsworth had expressed their reservations about specifying, in the body of the text, that there should be no "ex post facto laws" — no laws that made acts illegal after their commission, or that later enlarged the penalties attaching to the act. Their reservations did not spring from any uncertainty about ex post facto laws. Their concern, rather, was with the embarrassment that might be caused in the circles of the urbane by mentioning one or two principles of this kind and omitting others. Ellsworth remarked that "there was no lawyer, no civilian who would not say that *ex post facto* laws were void in themselves." And Wilson warned that "it will bring reflections on the Constitution — and proclaim that we are ignorant of the first principles of Legislation, or are constituting a Government which will be so." [9]

The American founders could set upon the task of framing a constitution precisely because they could take guidance from principles of constitutionalism that, they believed, existed independent of human will. They knew in the first place that a government restrained by law was morally superior to despotism. The principles of lawfulness enjoined the kind of government they were obliged to establish, and those principles gave them further guidance about the conventions and structures of that government. The founding generation might have been split into different factions as they drew out the implications of these principles. They were notably divided in their estimates of having an Executive with monarchical powers, or a government with more powers concentrated at the national level. But on the point that there were indeed principles of lawfulness, or what Wilson called "rational principles" of law, there was no serious division among either the Federalists or the Antifederalists. Which is to say, the American government began with the awareness of principles of right that did not depend merely on the "positive law."

Wilson's synthesis of America's dispute with Blackstone was the basis of the very first case that brought forth a set of opinions from the new Supreme Court, *Chisholm vs. Georgia*, in 1793.[10] In his own opinion, Wilson acknowledged that the judges could not rely solely on precedents but instead must observe "the principles of general jurisprudence." He was moved to explain the critical differences that separated the law in America from the law in England, and made the law in America entirely new. The law in England began with the "sovereign"; it was built on the principle "that all human law must be prescribed by a *superior.*" But the law in America would begin "with another principle, very different in its nature and operations." Jurisprudence would find here an entirely different ground: "Laws derived from the pure source of equality and justice must be founded on the consent of those, whose obedience they require. The sovereign, when traced to his source, must be found in the *man.*"[11]

Still, to replace "the sovereign" with "man" might simply supply another formula to suit the arrangements of legal positivism. An artless positivist might just accept as sovereign law the stipulations made by the aggregate of "men" — the rule of the majority. Wilson's alternative to Blackstone allowed that "man" could be "sovereign," but only insofar as his higher nature ruled over his lower nature and his appetites were governed by reason. In short, as Plato had it, the man who bore within himself a just constitutional order might justly rule others.

During the debates in Philadelphia over the ratification of the Constitution, Wilson was finally stung by what he took to be the cynicism that fueled its opponents. It was one thing to be aware that human beings were forked creatures, often given to self-love and low motives. Worldly men, who took human beings as they found them, would be properly guarded about the kinds of powers they would be willing to place in the hands of such creatures. But Wilson was moved to remark that, as he listened to the debates, the objections to the Constitution seemed to depend on a reading of human nature as unrelievedly evil. The warnings posted by one Antifederalist speaker about the dangers lurking in the legislature seemed to be predicated on the assumption that it would be an "association of demons." There was an extravagant willingness to assume that politicians would be inclined to be oppressive even when they had no particular interest to be advanced by that oppression.[12] Wilson harbored no illusions about human nature; he no doubt shared the sentiment expressed by Madison in *Federalist* 51 that "if men were angels, no government would be necessary."[13] But he understood, in the tradition running back to Aristotle and Plato, that we had polity and law precisely because human beings were neither beasts nor gods. A part of every human being is beastly, while another is attuned to the divine.

Machiavelli offered Chiron as the tutor to princes precisely because, as a centaur, he was half-man, half-beast.[14] No part of Chiron had anything to do with the gods. According to Machiavelli, political man would have to summon passions of a primordial, animal nature, not modulated or restrained by a more humane nature — let alone a godly one. By contrast, the founders understood with a sober realism that polity is necessary precisely because human beings require the restraints of law. But they also understood, with no less sobriety, that polity is possible only because human nature does not cut us off from the moral teaching that must be implicit in the law. And so, in a sweep of conviction both sober and romantic, Jefferson could observe that there was nothing beyond the will of the majority — except the moral law itself.[15]

The sweep of the assertion was a measure of that confidence, widely accepted as a matter of course among the generation of founders, that there is a moral law accessible to any reasonable being. Even a majority swept by the passion of partisanship could be expected to have at least that sense of principle necessary to guard their own enduring interests. Even in the throes of success, they would not be deaf to the concern that they might be establishing a precedent that could one day cut against their own rights.

We see an example of what they had in mind in the politics of our day. The temporary return from political death of Sen. Robert Packwood (Republican of Oregon) between 1993 and 1995 occasioned no small wonder. Senator Packwood seemed to be headed inexorably toward a political grave as a result of charges of "sexual harassment" from a remarkable plurality of sources. And yet when President Clinton himself came under comparable charges, Democrats in the Senate apparently came to this disquieting recognition: anything they said to confirm "sexual harassment" as an offense of the highest order — as a fault of character so deep as to disqualify man from public office — would undercut their defense of their own president. The case may move us to notice once again that human beings — even the species known as *Homo politicus* — cannot entirely avoid consistency about moral principle. To indict Senator Packwood while treating as utterly trivial the same charges leveled against a president of their own party would convict anyone of violating the elementary sense of fairness that is part of the foundation of the American regime. Senator Packwood was ultimately disposed of by his own party as an embarrassment. The founders, even more than their successors in the city of Washington, suffered no serious doubts about the "principles of lawfulness" that underlie our regime. For that reason, they could not be legal or moral "positivists." And for that reason, too, they could not fit readily into the cast of characters designed by Machiavelli.

The political man who *does* fit them was described with precision by Shakespeare in his rendering of Richard III. Richard needs no manual to direct him in staging the false appearances of virtue; nor does he suffer any inhibitions in the uses of cruelty. He orders up murders as they suit his purposes without a hint of reluctance. Shakespeare etches the outlines of this Machiavellian ruler also through the philosophic shading of lesser characters. Early in the play, Richard orders the murder of Clarence, before he can be pardoned by King Edward for his part in an insurrection. For this purpose Richard engages two men whom Shakespeare describes simply as "1. Murderer" and "2. Murderer." Shakespeare puts in their mouths the most moving exposition of the difference between the natural law and the positive law. When Clarence warns his killers that "the deed you undertake is damnable," Murderer 1 asserts that "what we will do, we do upon command." Murderer 2 echoes, "And he that hath commanded is our king." Clarence reminds them that there is another Sovereign, higher yet, who is the source of a Law that takes precedence over the commands of earthly kings.

> ... the great King of Kings
> Hath in the table of his law commanded
> That thou shalt do no murder. Will you then
> Spurn at his edict, and fulfil a man's?[16]

When Murderer 2 urges Clarence to "make peace with God, for you must die," Clarence retorts:

> Have you that holy feeling in your souls
> To counsel me to make my peace with God,
> And are you yet to your own souls so blind
> That you will war with God by murd'ring me?[17]

Clarence appeals to the murderers to "relent, and save your souls. . . . Not to relent is beastly, savage, devilish." Murderer 2 is evidently touched by these appeals. Clarence spies "some pity in thy looks." And indeed, the man that Shakespeare identifies only by his sinful vocation finally backs away from the deed. He makes a gesture at the last moment to jolt Clarence away from the stab he is about to receive, but it is too late. When the deed is done, the first murderer rebukes his partner: "What mean'st thou that thou help'st me not? By heavens, the duke shall know how slack you have been." Murderer 1 takes the high moral plane as the worker faithful to his mission. In the world of positive law, the man with moral inhibitions is nothing but a slacker. The hapless murderer, however, has moved to another plane of life. He wishes that, like Pilate, he could "wash my hands / Of this most grievous murder." He wishes, finally, to repent and in so doing registers his own recognition of an authority beyond Richard, and trembles at a punishment against which Richard, with all of the trappings of legal authority, can confer no immunity.

Legal positivism and cultural relativism are, as Henry James would say, merely chapters in the same book. Only an indistinct line separates them from moral conventionalism — the persuasion that our moral understanding is the product simply of the conventions or manners that spring up from place to place. As the saying goes these days, moral understandings are "socially constructed" from one locale to another, according to the vagaries of what is called the "local culture." The common theme that threads through all of these persuasions is the passion to deny that there are any "natural rights" or moral truths grounded in nature.

What, then, would a thoroughly anti-Machiavellian politics and an anti-Machiavellian politician look like? And would they be able to survive in a world filled with people who, as Machiavelli tells us, are "not good"? Consider Alexander Hamilton, and begin with a pamphlet he wrote as an eighteen-year-old student at King's College, in defense of the American revolution and "natural rights." Though written in white heat, as part of the political contest of the day, the pamphlet was nothing less than an attack on moral conventionalism and a critique of Thomas Hobbes, the writer who must stand closest to Machiavelli as the founder of "modern" politics. Hamilton saw, quite accurately, that "moral obligation, according to

[Hobbes], is derived from the introduction of civil society; and there is no virtue, but what is purely artificial, the mere contrivance of politicians, for the maintenance of social intercourse." Hamilton was no less precise in grasping the central point of corruption in the argument: "The reason [Hobbes] ran into this absurd and impious doctrine, was, that he disbelieved the existence of an intelligent superintending principle, who is the governor, and will be the final judge of the universe. . . . Good and wise men, in all ages, have embraced a very dissimilar theory. They have supposed, that the deity, from the relation we stand in, to himself and to each other, has constituted an eternal and immutable law, which is, indispensibly, obligatory upon all mankind, *prior to any human institution whatever.*" [18]

The American founders have been credited with the savviness of worldly men who had the nerve to steer a new, relatively weak nation through the hazards of international diplomacy. Had they been timid, or credulous and innocent of the world, they could not have accomplished this. And yet it should be clear from their writings that men like Washington, Hamilton, Wilson, and John Jay rejected the teachings of Machiavelli and Hobbes at their moral root. Nor was the rejection merely rhetorical; it would be hard to account for their policies and careers without that clarity about the grounds of their judgments. Nevertheless, nothing in that detachment seemed to impair them from operating in a world of diplomacy with high stakes and vivid dangers. Talleyrand remarked in his memoirs that he considered Napoléon, Charles James Fox, and Hamilton the three greatest men of the era; and among the three, he gave the first place to Hamilton, without hesitation.[19] So what it is that allowed these Americans to match wits with the world's most seasoned statesmen? Was it a capacity to set aside their moral judgments and turn Machiavellian when they had to? No, rather, they showed us once again what Aristotle had meant by "prudence."

Fourteen years after Hamilton wrote his precocious pamphlet — and after his service in the revolutionary war and the framing of the Constitution — he stood as the preeminent minister in the administration of George Washington. He was, nominally, secretary of the treasury. But Washington sought his counsel across the full breadth of the questions that arose for the first government under the new Constitution. Hamilton would rise above the attorney general in offering guidance to Washington on questions of constitutionality, and even on matters of foreign policy his counsel other proved more decisive than that of the secretary of state. Any of the crises that brought forth his judgments could be taken as a measure of his statesmanship, from the question of neutrality between Britain and France to relations with Saint-Domingue (now Haiti).[20] Any of his writings, over a long train of cases, could serve rather well to reflect his understanding; but I would focus here on a remarkable memorandum of foreign affairs that has drawn scant attention.

In the early fall of 1790, the British ambassador, Lord Dorchester, had delivered a note seeking permission to march British troops through American territory, from Detroit to the Mississippi, to engage the forces of Spain near the mouth of that river. The matter was freighted with hazards for weak America. Simply by granting the British request, the United States could become an accomplice in the injury of the Spanish. Conversely, by refusing to grant permission, the Americans could furnish a grievance to the British. President Washington requested Hamilton's advice.

Hamilton's reflex was to draw first on the classic commentators on international law: Barbeyrac, Pufendorf, Grotius, and especially Vatel. From Vatel the young Hamilton had learned both the "laws of nations" and the natural law.[21] For Vatel, justice in such matters involved either "innocent passage," by which a country may grant foreign troops the privilege of transit without concerning itself with the results, or "just occasion," in which a country may allow the transit of foreign troops for purposes of which it approves. But "innocent passage" would be a thin veil behind which to hide, because in the world of nations each government is held responsible for the judgments it makes about the just uses of its own territory. And with that responsibility comes danger.

Because the infant republic could not justly be expected to go to war against a superior power, international law might cover America's weakness with a release from obligation — but only on paper. In reality, if the United States lacked the strength to resist the British, that want of strength would in turn furnish an excuse to the Spanish. America could assert its independence by refusing the use of its territory to either party; but if it could not summon the strength to enforce its edict, it would expose itself to contempt. Its "independence" would then be reduced to a legal facade without substance.

For the sake of placating the Spanish, the British could be countered by bringing the weight of the French to bear on the side of America once again. This might be doable because, as Hamilton noted, the conduct of France, in relation to the United States, "bore the marks of liberal polity." Between the United States and France there remained a treaty of friendship, and the French were similarly connected to the Spanish. Still, it had to be supposed that the French were guided by a sober reckoning of their own interests. The French, wrote Hamilton, should not be counted on to rush to the side of

America, on any occasion, for any interest, in a sweep of romantic sentiment. As for the Spanish, Hamilton observed with a cool realism that "the
ally of our ally has no claim, as such, to our friendship." [22]

In fact, the Spanish had but "slender claims to peculiar good will from
us." The Spanish had never acknowledged the jural existence of the United
States. Indeed, they had maintained possessions within the territory claimed
by the United States, and without the consent of the Americans. They
refused to undertake treaties of commerce, and they actively used their
leverage over the Mississippi to obstruct the efforts of Americans to share
the navigation of that river.[23]

Ironically, this policy of the Spanish strengthened the hand of the British. For if the Spanish could cut off English-speaking settlers in the West
from their access to markets, these Americans might well seek the protection of the British. But that appeal would become more powerful yet if the
British managed to acquire the possessions of Spain and France in the
Floridas and Louisiana. The British would be contiguous to a larger part of
the American territory, with an undivided influence over the Indian tribes.
Hamilton saw the prospective danger as nothing less than "the dismember-
ment of the Western Country": "This will arise as well from the greater
power of annoying us, as from the different policy, which it is likely would
be pursued by [Britain], if in possession of the key to the only outlet for the
productions of that Country. Instead of shutting, they would probably open
the door to its inhabitants, and by conciliating their good will on the one,
hand and making them sensible on the other of their dependence on them
for the continuance of so essential an advantage they might hold out to them
the most powerful temptation to a desertion of their connection with the rest
of the United States. The avarice and ambition of individuals may be made
to cooperate in favour of these views." [24]

Only seven years had passed since the vindication of American independence, and one year since the country had been united under the new
Constitution. Patriotic sentiment held the country together. But Hamilton
understood, as fully as the drafters of the Declaration, that the concern for
safety, and the weight of "interest," could still overbear the sentiments that
attach people even to decent government.

If the Spanish persisted in barring the Americans from the use of the
Mississippi, the situation would lead "infallibly," as Hamilton wrote, to a
"War with Spain, or separation of the Western Country." But war with
Spain would bring the United States into opposition with France and make
it necessary to seek the aid of the British. That war, when the country was

prepared for it, would be preferable, he thought, to the existing state of affairs. And yet a war of that kind would have to "effect a revolution in the state of our foreign politics."[25]

Between the Spanish, then, and the British there was little to choose — unless, by taking sides with one against the other, the United States could secure one of its own vital interests: the government might negotiate a withdrawal of the British from the western posts or a recession of the Spanish from their obstruction of the Mississippi. However desirable, that goal was beyond America's power. Above all, it was crisply clear to Hamilton that the United States was simply not in a condition to wage war against any substantial European power. The American people were just recovering from a "long arduous and exhausting war." They were "vulnerable both by water and land without either fleet or army." They bore a considerable debt; their financial affairs were just becoming manageable. Measures had only recently been undertaken to restore the national credit, "which a war could hardly fail to disconcert and which if disturbed would be fatal to the means of prosecuting it." The national government was in its infancy, and in truth the people in many parts of the country were not domesticated to the habits of governance or the paying of taxes. All of these things conspired to make a war more expensive and more difficult to carry on. There was, among all classes, a "general disinclination" to war. "The theories of the speculative and the feelings of all are opposed to it."[26]

As Hamilton weighed the strands of the problem against this background, he distilled this judgment: "The acquisition of the Spanish territories, bordering upon the U States, by Britain would be dangerous to us. And if there were a good prospect that our refusal would prevent it, without exposing us to a greater evil, we ought to refuse. But if there be a considerable probability that our refusal would be ineffectual, and if being so, it would involve us in war or disgrace, and if positive disgrace is worse than war, and war, in our present situation, worse, than the chances of the evils, which may befall us, from that acquisition then the conclusion would be that we ought not to refuse."[27]

This judgment could be enhanced by the happy accident that dangers, often so acute in prospect, turn out to be much diminished in fact. The British might not prove deft in carrying out their enterprise. They might find it expedient then to purchase the good will of the United States by ceding a portion of the territory in question, which bordered on the Mississippi. In the meantime, the British could be adding millions to their debt, while the

Americans, minding their own business, would see each day of peace adding to their resources and strength.

Might there be — as Hamilton put the question — "a middle course between refusal and consent"? Could the United States simply avoid giving offense to either side by decorously stepping back from an explicit decision one way or the other? But that course was likely to be taken as a sign of timidity and to elicit contempt in both camps. In any case, the British would likely be impelled to press on and force a decision. As Hamilton noted, there was an American post on the Wabash River, which the British expedition was likely to pass. The commanding officer of the post, with no orders to the contrary, would be obliged to put up a resistance. Thus a policy of silence was likely to produce the worst of all worlds: British troops would be passing through American territory without consent, and the United States would be drawn into a war that it had no interest in inviting.

As Hamilton summed up the matter, the government could not hold back in indecision, and the most prudent decision, on balance, was to grant consent to the British. Still, it should be granted with hedges and warnings — with "a candid intimation that the expedition is not agreeable to us, but that thinking it expedient to avoid an occasion of controversy, it has been concluded not to withhold assent." And at the same time, "an early and frank explanation should be given to Spain."

But the president had posed to Hamilton a second, related question: What if the British decided to press on with their expedition without asking further leave, or before the American government could arrive at a judgment? Hamilton thought that the response, even here, could turn on circumstances. If the British traveled through the Great Lakes, through an uninhabited part of the country, they would not come into collision with Americans. In that event, the United States could enter a remonstrance, but not the kind that would commit the country to war.

On the other hand, if the British moved along the Wabash, they would encounter an American garrison. At that point, wrote Hamilton, "there seems no alternative but to go to war with them; unwelcome as it may be." Hamilton had described it earlier as "a *sound maxim* that a state had better hazard any calamities than submit tamely to absolute disgrace."[28] There seemed to be, in short, a matter of national honor; and in the face of that decisive test, all of the hesitations, all of the discounts and cautions and hedgings, were suddenly swept away, like a vast clearing of the mind. And as Hamilton reached the culmination of his paper, his advice to his chief reached a point singularly free of qualification: "In such an event, it would appear advisable immediately to convene the Legislature; to take the most vigorous measures for war; to make formal demand of satisfaction; to commence negotiations for alliances; and if satisfaction should be refused to endeavour to punish the aggression by the sword." [29]

This was not a memorandum struck off in the style of some American state papers of late, by an official whose knowledge of war came mainly from social science models and board games. The memorandum was informed, at every point, by experience and by a profound realism. In that respect, it suffers in no comparison with the sophistication that Machiavelli would offer for the instruction of a prince. But it should be quite as evident that the writer could not have been identified even remotely as a Machiavellian or a "Hobbesian."

Modern natural right was anchored firmly in the premise of "self-preservation." Hence, for the true Hobbesian it was always incoherent to ask someone to risk his life for the larger good of the community, let alone for an abstraction like "honor." For in Hobbes's understanding, a person wills the state into existence for his own self-preservation, not the preservation of others. A government might try to deploy its citizens on the beaches of Normandy, with shells exploding all about, but it was implausible to pretend that this exercise had, as its object, the self-preservation of each soldier. That is why, in the strictest reckoning, there could never be, in Hobbes's teaching, an "obligation" to serve in the military.[30] "When armies fight," said Hobbes, "there is on one side, or both, a running away." Hobbes was immanently prepared to honor the claim of the soldier who was governed by the first law of nature and fled from battle out of fear for his life. When soldiers flee "not out of treachery, but fear, they are not esteemed to do it unjustly." [31] He described such soldiers as acting out of cowardice, not injustice; they are acting not "unjustly, but dishonourably." But when self-preservation became the ground of moral judgment, the terms "cowardice" and "dishonor" were evacuated of their moral significance. If the act of running away was not unjustified or wrong, then cowardice or dishonor merely described timidity or caution in battle. They would no longer mark anything truly shameful or wrong.

The true — or at any rate the most honest — Hobbesian man on the field of battle was Shakespeare's Falstaff. That ribald, profligate figure was surely the most reluctant of soldiers. When he was prodded by Prince Hal ("thou owest God a death"), he remarked of that "debt" that " 'Tis not due yet, I would be loath to pay him before his day — what need I be so forward with him that calls not on me." Still, he offers, " 'tis no matter, honor pricks me on":

Yea, but how if honour prick me off when I
come on, how then? Can honour set to a leg?
No. Or an arm? No. Or take away the grief of
a wound? No. Honour hath no skill in
surgery then? No. What is honour? A word.
What is in that word honour? What is that
honour? Air. A trim reckoning! Who hath
it? He that died a-Wednesday. Doth he feel
insensible, then? Yea, to the dead. But
will it not live with the living? No. Why?
Detraction will not suffer it. Therefore I'll
none of it.[32]

Falstaff may cut a laughable figure, but on one point he is impeccable as
a philosopher: Honor does not belong to the world of sensation and matter.
He who died a-Wednesday surely does not "feel" it. But then, of course,
none of those understandings that provide a moral substance to our lives are
known to us through the world of "sensation." The evil that men do may be
measured empirically, but there is nothing essentially empirical about "justice," "equity," "fairness." They do not make an impression on our retinas,
or on any other of our senses. We do not see Inequities walking down the
street, or Obligations falling out of trees. In our cultivated understanding,
we may say that we "sense" the presence of a self-serving argument, but we
do not literally touch or smell a bad argument. It was Hobbes who advanced
the revolution begun by Machiavelli, and Hobbes thought that if a hurt is
not "corporeal," it must be "phantastical." The concern for "honor was
disparaged, along with the concern for the terms of principle on which lives
are preserved."

Machiavelli himself showed no deficit of spirit or pride, or love of
honor. But he taught that men could be elevated in politics as a result of
doing things that were either noble or base; and that the honors of office, the
pride and prestige of power, have no moral requirements. Attaining supreme power is an achievement sufficiently worthy of our respect in and of
itself. That princes might have made their way to the heights of power by
doing grisly things, or that they might use their power for debased ends,
does not concern the science of politics bequeathed to us by Machiavelli.[33]
As we have seen, however, America's founding fathers connected honor
with what is naturally noble as tightly as they could. So, in that critical
respect, America is as unmodern, as anti-Machiavellian as could be.

The founders of the social sciences, by contrast, are very much Machiavelli's heirs. American social scientists take pride in detaching their judgments from moral judgments of ends or of character. The typical line of social scientists is "Do you have any empirical evidence for that?" Like Falstaff on the field of battle, they live in the world of "sensation" and "matter." They will not speak of things amoral or immoral, just or unjust, but only of the things that can be confirmed or falsified with empirical evidence. The social scientists of politics may map with painstaking precision the opinions that move people to support nazism or communism. But their science has nothing to say about whether there is anything wrongful or corrupting in these political choices. Though political scientists vocation — and claim — is to shed light on politics, they cannot illuminate the most profound choices that human beings may make about their political ends.

Armed with this understanding of his vocation, that most excellent of political scientists, Robert Dahl, set off years ago to offer an account of the conditions of democracy in an American city. And although no one could gainsay Dahl's passion for democracy, neither could one mistake the fact that, as social scientist, he was preserving his ultimate detachment as to the goodness or rightness of democracy. In all strictness, he would not profess to "know" that democracy stood on a higher moral plane than "despotism," with a superior claim to anyone's respect. Like Machiavelli, he would preserve the most scrupulous detachment on the question of virtue and vice.

Dahl did ask how one would go about preserving a democratic regime (on the assumption that *someone* might think it worth preserving). Dahl was aware of the traditional answer, that current and future citizens must be taught the old "self-evident" truths that explain why it is wrong to rule human beings in the way that humans properly rule horses and dogs. It could be explained that beings who can give and understand reason deserved to be ruled through a government that offers reasons as it seeks their consent. The account could be amplified by explaining once more the principles of lawfulness — principles like the ban on ex post facto laws — in short, the principles of constitutional government. When all these reasons were brought together, they explained to citizens just why they were obliged to choose and preserve this form of government, or why they were obliged to honor the equal rights of others, even when these arrangements might not serve their interests.

Like every student of politics running back to Aristotle, Dahl saw the obvious utility in this civic instruction. But unlike Aristotle, he did not see it as instruction. Rather, he described this regimen of civic education as "indoctrination."[34] After all, in his view the moral preference for democracy could not be grounded in a knowable truth. It had to rest, then, on belief or opinion. A "belief" was a conviction based ultimately on uncertain or imperfect knowledge, and it was irreducibly "personal." No belief stood on a higher epistemic plane than any other belief. The beliefs that sustained liberal democracy had no higher claim to be true than the beliefs that supported Marxist dictatorships.

The contrast with the more ancient, or classical, understanding of politics would come into view more readily if we were to ask: Do we "indoctrinate" students in the rudiments of mathematics or in the Pythagorean theorem? Or do we rather "teach" them truths? And does that teaching not become ever more compelling as we lead them to the theorems through the axioms on which they are built? After all, our confidence in the truth of the theorems arises directly from the fact that they rest on axioms that are self-evident to anyone who understands them.

But the familiar response — tendered in milliseconds — is that of course politics cannot be likened to mathematics. And yet, the American founders quite as much as the ancient teachers of politics understood both politics and mathematics as founded on objective truth. Plato thought that geometry was indeed an apt preparation for anyone who hoped to grasp the axioms and principles of moral reasoning. As for the founders, they made it amply clear in their writings — at times even in comments thrown off in passing[35] — that their knowledge of matters moral and political found its ground in axioms and "self-evident" truths along with anything else they would claim to know.

No one expressed this understanding with more clarity and elegance than Hamilton in the opening paragraph of *Federalist* 31. The subject of that paper was taxation. But Hamilton offered a telling illustration of the mind that his generation brought even to the most prosaic matters. Hamilton framed the problem by reminding his readers in the first place that "in disquisitions of every kind there are certain primary truths, or first principles, upon which all subsequent reasonings must depend. These contain an internal evidence which, antecedent to all reflection or combination, command the assent of the mind. . . . Of this nature are the maxims in geometry that the whole is greater than its parts; that things equal to the same are equal to one another; that two straight lines cannot enclose in space; and that all right angles are equal to each other. Of the same nature are these other maxims in ethics and politics, that there cannot be an effect without a cause; that the means ought to be proportioned to the end; that every power ought to be commensurate with its object; that there ought to be no limitation of a power destined to effect a purpose which is itself incapable of limitation." [36]

A class of political men who could write in this way about the grounds of their own judgments deserved the name of founders, for they could be luminously clear about the root premises and character of the regime they were founding. They could give an account of that regime, and they would suffer no doubts about the first principles in which the case for that regime would be anchored.

It has been aptly said that the founders stood outside the American regime in the way that the rest of us, the children of that regime, cannot. The structure of the Constitution has become, for us, part of the landscape, and we have often absorbed its premises, or its leading maxims, as though they were now part of our own natures. And yet, in recent years it has become evident that this is no longer the case. The conventions of the Constitution have become familiar, but the deeper principles of the regime, the principles that the founders could explain with pristine clarity, have now evaporated from the understanding of the American political class, largely replaced by the principles of the social science founded by Machiavelli.

This melancholy point was brought home to me recently in an account offered by a friend, who was teaching at a war college attached to one of our military services. His students were all seasoned veterans, in their forties. They had all seen military action; but they had been college students in the late 1960s, and they had absorbed much of the secular religion that affected other young people in those years. They had risked their lives for their country, but they were far from clear that there was anything about the American republic that truly justified what they had done. They were sceptical that moral truths remain true in all times and places. They could not really say, with Lincoln, that the right of human beings to govern themselves is "applicable to all men at all times." These soldiers of the country of the Declaration of Independence were more disposed to believe, with the professors who taught them in college, that right and wrong are always contingent, always "relative" to the "culture" or the country in which it is held. They would not claim, then, that the political regime in America was morally superior to the institutions in the Soviet Union or Vietnam. They settled for the far more modest claim that our political way of life was at least "ours": it was consistent with our traditions—it was "right," we might say, *for us*, and on that basis we were warranted in hazarding our lives to preserve it.

In this sense, of course, the principles of the American republic would be no different from the rules of a club, or the rules that define any sport: the rules of the American Constitution are of the same order as the rules of baseball or the rules of chess. In that event, as I pointed out to my friend, the willingness of his students to risk their lives for the rules of the American republic apparently stood on the same moral plane as a willingness to risk one's life to preserve baseball's infield fly rule, or its institution of the designated hitter.[37]

Clearly, these officers were not the spiritual descendants of Hamilton. The maxims they had absorbed as their deep principles of politics were not those of the American founders. So whose descendants were these officers? Or, to put it another way, who was the founder of the regime of which they would stand now as the protectors? Plainly, these Americans were the intellectual descendants of professors, in or out of the academy, who taught that the question of loyalty to the laws could be severed from the moral content of those laws—from the question of whether those laws truly merited respect. Regardless of whether that teaching reached them through social science, legal realism, or even literary deconstruction, its roots are in ancient scepticism and its dramatic application to matters political is from Machiavelli and his successors.

It might be said that, in the move from the ancients to the moderns, there was a "refounding" of political philosophy. And the man who propelled the movement saw himself distinctly as a founder, even though he held no political office. Leo Strauss remarked of *The Prince* that the "peaks" were deliberately missing: Machiavelli cited passages from the Old Testament but not from the New. His references to the Greek philosophers were to Xenophon; he conspicuously omitted Plato and Aristotle. Machiavelli himself would supply the missing high points; he would represent the completion of political thought, ancient and modern.[38]

Machiavelli taught, of course, that laws backed by good arms were better laws, and that the prophet armed was better than the prophet unarmed. Machiavelli was certainly aware that Jesus was the preeminent example of the prophet unarmed, and it must have been evident to him that he himself was a leading example of the prophet unarmed. As such, he sought nothing less than to rival Jesus. "Nothing is more difficult to transact," he wrote, in that passage often quoted, "nor more dubious to succeed, nor more dangerous to manage, than to make one's self chief to introduce new orders."[39] But at the same time, "nothing does so much honor to a man who newly arises, as do the new laws and the new orders founded by him."[40] The teacher of founders, the author of new political orders, is an even more sovereign founder yet.

The measure of Machiavelli's achievement may be found in the way that men have absorbed his premises and his teachings, even without knowing that they are his. And in this manner may the very axes of politics be turned: Our angle of vision may be altered, and with it our sense of the subjects that come into view when we speak of the proper business of political life. In our own time, it has become common to speak of the so-called social issues in politics. By that we seem to mean abortion, the family, homosexuality, the place of religion in our public life. Why are these things set apart as not exactly, or not properly, "political"? The label suggests that they are rather exotic, peripheral to the main, legitimate questions of politics. And what is the apt business of our political leaders? Why, prosperity, growth and unemployment, taxes and regulation; in short, "managing the economy."

Yet the American founders, with all their accomplishments, never pretended to "manage the economy." They claimed a decent knowledge of political economy, an understanding of the moral principles that bore on the economy and affected the distribution of property. They understood that the passion of injustice would often employ genius in finding ever more subtle ways to confiscate the property of others, or to secure benefits at the expense of someone else. But apart from laying precautions against these kinds of temptations, the founders did not fashion a national government that claimed the power, or the competence, to manage the economy. The framers did not profess to know just what distributions of privilege would in principle be more "just." Nor did they claim possession of a causal science of economics, which would invest them with the privileged knowledge of how to manipulate the supply of money and public spending for the sake of producing prosperity and a "just" distribution. This agnosticism may help explain why the American economy quickly became the world's wonder. The claim of knowledge about how to manage an economy was no part of traditional "political economy." It is a claim that arose along with modern economics as a species of social science.

The project of government has been redefined in our own time to coincide with the project of social science, which claims to know far more than the founders and at the same time far less. The limits of Machiavellian social science should be clear enough. If government officials advised by the very best social scientists could guarantee benign results, no president need ever suffer the embarrassment of running for office with an economy less than buoyant. But the fact that governments repeatedly prove incompetent in this regard does nothing to dislodge the superstition that there exists a science by which governments may discharge their responsibility for directing the economy. And that sense of a responsibility that can neither be met nor avoided seems merely to spur politicians and their advisers to spending, taxing, and tinkering without logical end.

Machiavelli himself, however, set a practical limit to economic management:

> In the end, if he wants to retain the name of liberal, [a prince] will be required to weigh down the people extraordinarily and to be taxy and to do all the things that can be done in order to have money. This will begin to make him hateful to the subjects . . . ; so that, having hurt the many and rewarded the few with this liberality of his, he feels every least unrest . . . ; when he realizes this and waiting to pull back from it, he right away incurs the infamy of the miser. Therefore, since a prince cannot use this virtue of liberality without damage to himself, if he is prudent, he must not worry about the reputation of a miser; because with time he will be considered as even more liberal, when it is seen that because of his parsimony his income suffices him. . . . By which token he comes to use liberality toward all those from whom he does not take, who are infinite, and miserliness toward all to whom he does not give, who are few.[41]

In modern American politics, Machiavelli's practical advice is a truer guide than the social science of which Machiavelli is the father. A government primed to rush to the relief of its citizens, in all of their descriptions, suddenly finds an ongoing parade of victims: workers at Chrysler or Caterpillar, faced with the loss of their jobs; farmers vulnerable to falling incomes and the loss of their farms; denizens of Florida suffering the wreckage of a hurricane; young people without medical insurance courting the hazards of life—all have acquired the habit of expecting a remedy at the hands of the government. But in order to furnish any remedy, the government must tax the very people to whom it gives.

Contrary to Machiavelli's practical advice, social scientists think that this sort of activity strengthens governments. Yet this attitude is consistent with the Machiavellian root of their science, by which the strength of governments, the force of law, derives from the manipulation of threats and promises rather than from moral consensus.

The founders understood that the principal mission of government was to secure people in their natural rights—to protect them against the lawless assault on their lives and arbitrary restriction of their freedom, on the part of private thugs as well as of ill-intentioned legislators. But now, with a high rate of crime and violence, the government seems afraid to mobilize the population against it by appealing to the wrongness of crimes and the responsibility of criminals. Instead, it seeks to "prevent" crimes by manipulating social conditions. This passion persists even while its programs persistently fail to solve, or even to ameliorate, the problem of crime.

The modern project in politics, the project launched by Machiavelli and Hobbes, has sought to deliver people in power from the vexing discipline of framing their acts in moral terms. That state of mind has reached an exquisite refinement in modern jurisprudence, and no voice of that jurisprudence has been clearer than that of Justice Oliver Wendell Holmes, who thought it would be a decided gain "if every word of moral significance could be banished from the law altogether." [42] In this jurisprudence, the measures of government pass the test of constitutionality only if their purposes can be translated in terms that are safely nonmoral. And so, when the state of Indiana passed a statute barring nude entertainment, Holmes was heard again through his current epigone, Justice David Souter. Souter was willing to sustain this law only on the supposition that the law is directed to certain "secondary effects" that may be generated by such excitements, namely, prostitution, increased numbers of sexual assaults, or other crimes. [43] It fell to Chief Justice William Rehnquist to make the simple, ineffaceable point that the law had to be accepted or rejected on its own terms: the "moral disapproval of people appearing in the nude among strangers in public places." [44]

The aspiration of Holmes, to detach morality from law, may explain the contemporary reflex to detach the estimate of a public man from the evidence of what is called his "private morality." This reflex consigns morality to the private realm, as though it were largely irrelevant to anyone's capacity to discharge the public business. In the mid-1990s that argument has been unfurled to cover a president whose passion for private adventures begot a stream of public embarrassments, which began to spill over into the public business. One of the more telling spills occurred in the case mentioned above, of Sen. Bob Packwood.

Packwood had been placed in the dock of public accusation as a result of a string of incidents with women, which brought forth charges of sexual harassment. In the aftermath of the confrontation between Anita Hill and Clarence Thomas in 1991, politicians in Washington seemed driven to show that they regarded charges of sexual harassment as concerns of state so high that credible accusations would be tantamount to convictions, turn the accused into lepers, and automatically end their careers. Hence, Packwood had already become untouchable and his career seemed to be terminating. But a few months later the media had ceased to hound Packwood about sex and instead asked him polite, technocratic questions about health care reform. Why did so many, Democrats especially, suddenly become so much less zealous about sexual harassment? Democrats surely had a powerful incentive — their president himself had come under accusations of sexual harassment by Paula Jones which were at least as credible as the accusations against Packwood. Hence, the president's supporters in Congress had to look directly into the cameras and, with the ring of conviction, to repeat the old bromide that a man's private life should not enter into our judgments as we assess his handling of the public business.

That familiar refrain seemed to hold — except for one thing. Some remembered that these very people had labored over the previous two years to put sexual harassment at the very center of our *public* business. Happily, not even our species of politicians is so constituted that it can declaim on the high seriousness of sexual harassment in one room, and then, on the same day, in another room, insist that the matter is really peripheral to public life. Hence, supporters of the president seemed to resolve themselves quietly to supporting their president, and with the same delicacy they receded from pressing the issue of Senator Packwood.

But despite this delicacy, and even though Clinton's party withdrew from the position that sexual harassment is nothing less than a grave public matter, the president's nether life had diminished, gravely, his own and his party's moral authority and capacity to conduct the public business.[45] This might not have been so elsewhere in the modern world. But it is certainly so in America.

Most clearly in America, but also elsewhere, the tension between private lives and public duties cannot be dissolved simply by ignoring public issues that raise explicitly moral questions. This tension is one of those intractable facts rooted in our natures. Nothing in modernity has made the problem either more acute or less pressing. There is an enduring aptness, then, in W. H. Auden's lament at the grave of Henry James: "Master of nuance and scruple / Pray for me, and for all writers . . . / Because there are many whose works / Are in better taste than their lives."[46] Our own day is different only in that the reigning slogans give public figures an excuse for trying to turn away from distinctly moral questions.

But moral questions there must be. No one is capable of making it through the week, even in the most prosaic life, without praising or condemning, taking offense or offering approval, remarking about the aptness or ineptness of things; in short, casting judgments about the things that are right and wrong, just and unjust. And since we cannot evade moral judgments, we cannot evade the logic that moves us to cast those judgments in the form of laws. As Aristotle understood, laws spring from our natures, and they will always be pronouncing judgments on right and wrong. The only question is whether those judgments will be explicit or disguised: Will they be made openly, by legislators who are willing to take on the discipline of justifying their measures? Or will they be made by politicians who are altogether willing to impose their judgments on others with the force of law, even as they insist, with a cheerful assurance, that there are no foundations for those moral judgments?

No one who knows our politics, and the training ground of our lawyers and judges, will fail to recognize the latter type. Only in our age do we find the happy relativist, who is convinced that no person may speak about the things that are right and wrong for others, and yet is willing to exercise the levers of power with fondness for the game.

Again: this sort of thing merely hides moral judgment and makes it less subject to intellectual discipline. Immorality may come with shameless cruelties, but also with the artlessness of a civil servant or of an earnest candidate for office who aspires to the permanent tenure of a civil servant. With unbroken geniality, such politicians hand out pamphlets and bumper stickers at shopping centers, offering themselves to the voters as a provider of "services" to their constituents, while dulling their capacity to understand the moral choices involved in the election. Between cruelty and banality there may be merely a difference in style. "For Wales?" Thomas More could pose the question, without really asking, to the young man who was willing to sell him out for a scrap of patronage. "Why, Richard, it profits a man nothing to give his soul for the whole world. . . . But for Wales!" [47] One man might render a servile loyalty for the recompense of being the Keeper of the Buffalo Boxes, and another might seek the glory of battles and large projects, but a glory wholly disconnected from any concern for the things that make his ends just or unjust. The two may differ merely in scale.

Machiavelli advised his prince that "only those defenses are good, are certain, are durable, that depend on you yourself and on your virtue." [48] His word *virtù* placed the accent on skill and success, rather than on moral uprightness. But with a sublime accident, the reader who takes that word in its usual sense of "virtue" may learn a more accurate lesson. As our own experiences constantly remind us, politicians with discounted characters may find themselves disarmed more fully than unarmed prophets. Even bands of thieves know that much. Only in *The Prince*, the primer of modernity and realism, is this lesson muted. To account soberly for the political strength that accrues from real, not feigned, virtue may be a lesson far too startling to be received as plausible by the students of this new science of politics. In the politics shaped by Machiavelli, in the world we may inhabit even now, a realistic doctrine of virtue may have to be conveyed as a covert teaching. Unlike in Hamilton's day, virtue is not something that the urbane will proclaim openly and teach in public.

NOTES

1. Leo Strauss, *Thoughts on Machiavelli* (Glencoe, Ill., 1985), p. 9.

2. Strauss, *Natural Right and History* (Chicago, 1953), p. 160.

3. Strauss, *Thoughts on Machiavelli*, p. 13.

4. Quoted by Blackstone in *Commentaries on the Laws of England* (Oxford, 1765; repr. Chicago, 1979), I, 157.

5. Ibid.

6. Wilson, "First Lecture on the Law," in *The Works of James Wilson*, ed. Robert Green McCloskey (Cambridge, Mass., 1967; orig. pub. 1804), vol. 1, p. 79.

7. Cited by Wilson, ibid., p. 78.

8. Ibid.

9. Max Farrand, ed., *The Records of the Federal Convention of 1787* (New Haven, 1966), vol. 2, p. 376 [Aug. 22]. For a fuller discussion of the original argument over a bill of rights, see Arkes, *Beyond the Constitution* (Princeton, 1990), chap. 4.

10. 2 *Dallas* 419.

11. Ibid., at 458.

12. See Jonathan Eliot, *Debates in the Several State Conventions on the Adoption of the Constitution* (Philadelphia, 1859), vol. 2, pp. 486–87.

13. *The Federalist* (New York, n.d.), p. 337.

14. *The Prince* XVIII.

15. Jefferson was making the point, in a letter to Spencer Roane, that the ultimate authority for the meaning of the Constitution would rest with the people themselves, not with the Judiciary, or any other branch of the government: "Independence can be trusted nowhere but with the people in mass. They are inherently independent of all but moral law." Quoted by Harry V. Jaffa, *Original Intent and the Framers of the Constitution* (Washington, D.C., 1994), p. 287.

16. *Richard III*, act I, scene iv.

17. Ibid.

18. "The Farmer Refuted" (February 1775), in *The Papers of Alexander Hamilton*, ed. Harold C. Syrett (New York, 1961), vol. 1, pp. 86–87; emphasis added.

19. Talleyrand, "Etudes sur la Republique," cited in Allan McLane Hamilton, *The Intimate Life of Alexander Hamilton* (New York, 1910), p. 255.

20. For a fascinating account of the differences between Hamilton and Jefferson in their approach to the black republic, see Roger G. Kennedy, *Orders from France* (New York, 1989), pp. 140–42, 144, 145, 149, 162.

21. Emer de Vatel, *The Law of Nations or the Principles of Natural Law* (1757).

22. See the memorandum to Washington, Sept. 15, 1790, in *The Papers of Alexander Hamilton*, ed. Harold C. Syrett (New York, 1961), vol. 7, pp. 36–57, at 45.

23. Ibid., p. 44.

24. Ibid., p. 46.

25. Ibid., at 53.

26. Ibid., pp. 49–50.

27. Ibid., p. 54.

28. Ibid., p. 49; italics in original.

29. Ibid., pp. 56–57.

30. I argued this point with some care in *First Things* (Princeton, 1986), pp. 206–20.

31. Thomas Hobbes, *Leviathan* (Oxford, 1960 [1651]), chap. 21, p. 143.

32. *Henry IV*, Part I, act V, scene i.

33. See, in this vein, Strauss, *Thoughts on Machiavelli*, pp. 79–80.

34. See Robert A. Dahl, *Who Governs?* (New Haven, 1961), pp. 317, 319.

35. For some examples, see Arkes, *Beyond the Constitution*, pp. 27–28.

36. *Federalist* 31, p. 188.

37. I recalled this incident in "Moral Obtuseness in America" (review of the television series *Ethics in America*), *National Review*, June 16, 1989, pp. 33–36.

38. Strauss, *Thoughts on Machiavelli*, p. 59.

39. *The Prince* VI.

40. Ibid. XXVI.

41. Ibid. XVI.

On this, by now, familiar point, see James Q. Wilson, "What to Do about Crime," *Commentary*, September 1994, pp. 25–34.

42. Holmes, "The Path of the Law," in *Collected Legal Papers* (New York, 1920), p. 179.

43. See *Barnes v. Glen Theatre*, 115 L.Ed.2d 504, at 522, 524 (1991).

And on this problem more generally, see Arkes, *The Philosopher in the City* (Princeton, 1981), chap. 14 ("Law, Morals, and the Regulation of Vices").

44. Ibid., 512.

45. See "The Fall and Amazing Rise of Senator Bob Packwood," *New York Times*, July 10, 1994.

46. W. H. Auden, "At the Grave of Henry James," in *Collected Poems*, ed. Edward Mendelson (New York, 1976), p. 243.

47. Robert Bolt, *A Man for All Seasons* (New York, 1962; Vintage ed. 1990), p. 158.

48. *The Prince* XXIV.

Contributors

William B. Allen is dean, James Madison College, Michigan State University.

Hadley Arkes is Edward Ney Professor of American Institutions, Amherst College.

Angelo M. Codevilla is professor of International Relations, Boston University.

Carnes Lord is professor, Fletcher School of Law and Diplomacy, Tufts University.

Rethinking the Western Tradition

The Prince

NICCOLÒ MACHIAVELLI

Translated and edited by Angelo Codevilla,
with essays by Carnes Lord, W. B. Allen,
and Hadley Arkes

A classic of the Western tradition, Machiavelli's *The Prince* has influenced political and philosophical thought since its publication four centuries ago. Political power, Machiavelli taught, has no limits. It leaves no room for the sacred, and it subordinates right and wrong to success. In this new edition of Machiavelli's momentous book, Angelo Codevilla provides a translation uniquely faithful to the original, and especially sensitive to the author's use of verbal imprecision, including puns, double meanings, and the subjunctive mood.

The volume includes an introduction by Codevilla that places Machiavelli in the context of his own times, demonstrates his relevance to the history of political thought, and inquires into the place of Machiavelli's ideas in modern debates. This edition also contains three essays that explore some of the most important ways *The Prince* clashes with the other main branch of Western Civilization — the Socratic and Judeo-Christian traditions: "Machiavelli's Realism" by Carnes Lord, "Machiavelli and Modernity" by W. B. Allen, and "Machiavelli and America" by Hadley Arkes.

"Codevilla has the ability to convey in a straightforward and accessible style what is important about the Western Tradition and about Machiavelli's contribution to it." — Larry Peterman, University of California, Davis

RETHINKING THE WESTERN TRADITION SERIES